How to Put Yourself Across with Key Words and Phrases

HOW TO PUT YOURSELF ACROSS
WITH KEY WORDS AND PHRASES

MARTHA W. CRESCI

PARKER PUBLISHING COMPANY, INC.

West Nyack, N.Y.

Library of Congress Cataloging in Publication Data

Cresci, Martha W
   How to put yourself across with key words and
phrases.

  1. Success. I. Title.
BF637.S8C76   650'.13   73-17
ISBN 0-13-430678-3

Printed in the United States of America

Dedicated to my mother, *Olive Brems Weatherly,* who taught me early to seek out basic truths, and to view the world as a spectacle.

What This Book Can Do
For You

A perceptive person who has been in the business world for any length of time knows very well that the race is not always won by the swift, and that the most intelligent people or those with great ability are not always at the top. Sometimes people of seemingly huge potential never get a chance to show what they can do. Others get the chance and blow it; while a mediocre type goes onward and upward, often (quite properly) using the abilities of underlings to support his position.

Despite these observable facts, most books about getting ahead replay all the old saws. Even a recent best seller had as its main point, "Work hard. Do your job efficiently. The spectacle will be so amazing that you will stand out and will quickly be promoted." Balderdash! If this is all you do you will be *used*, but you will rarely be adequately rewarded. Worse yet, you may be resented and secretly sabotaged by your associates. Faint praise will mark you as "a good, solid worker; but without much personality . . . not managerial material . . . too bad . . . "

Beyond sufficient drive and a good knowledge of the job, beyond required degrees and minimal executive ability, what is it that sends one man or woman ahead, while another grits his teeth with frustration? Some people seem to be born with the answer. Others forever batter helplessly at doors that would open easily with the right key.

The book you now hold deals with the hard facts of business and professional life and gives you the real answers. Here you will find revealed the techniques of putting yourself across, the actual words and phrases that you can use to promote yourself from day to day. How to use them and when to use them is carefully explained, with examples drawn from experience.

Perhaps you have been told airily that the secret of success is the ability to get along with people. True enough, as far as that goes; but if you were not born with this gift, or did not learn it in your earliest years, the statement is a puzzle within a puzzle, and no help at all. You need to have the methods explained (there are methods). Actually, this ability to get along with people is only one factor in getting ahead. In order to succeed you must be able to put yourself across as an important person, as executive material. You must make people want to help you and push you. You must be able to avoid many traps and glide gracefully out of others, so that you project a favorable, successful image of yourself at all times.

How do you do it? HOW? Telling you exactly how is the purpose of this straightforward book.

The author's study of a vast parade of executives under every business condition, in every imaginable business situation, has revealed that the secrets of success, fully putting yourself across, are fairly simple. Indeed the secrets consist, by and large, of a collection of key words and phrases that shape the reactions of others. Happily, these are words and phrases that any reasonably intelligent person can learn, can practice in private, and use in public to achieve his ends.

Whatever your job and no matter how well you are doing, this study will prove a revelation to you. Some of the techniques you may even recognize. You will perhaps say to yourself, "Why, I've seen Jones do that, and I didn't even think about it as a technique!" Other key words and phrases will be new to you, but if you are wise you will make them your own.

Fortunes can be spent on training in various specialties, and yet, if the techniques of putting yourself across have not been learned, the full value of your training may never be realized. Knowledge is fine, but if you cannot put across the idea that you have it and can use it effectively, others will beat you to the rewards that should be yours.

The fact of the matter is that if it is possible, the key words and phrases should be learned first. They are the keys to making people listen happily to your ideas and opinions. They are the keys to the friendship of those who can boost you to the top. These key words and phrases make it easier to get and keep a job, to rise above the crowd wherever you are — yet without arousing opposition or resentment.

The art of putting yourself across is of primary importance to your business or profession, your enjoyment of your job. The monetary value is incalculable. At the same time, when you have learned these techniques so that the use of the key words and phrases becomes second nature, you will find them of benefit in every phase of life. The businessman will get along better with his firm. The businesswoman who learns them will find her importance increasing. Life on the whole, even in personal relationships, will be more successful, more pleasurable.

Anyone who has ever gotten off on the wrong foot in a discussion will find this book an eye-opener. How many times have you annoyed someone unintentionally with an ill-chosen or misunderstood remark, and then found that the more you tried to extricate yourself, the more embroiled you became? How many times have you seen Jones going off to play golf with the boss, while you get your kicks on the company bowling team? How many times have you seen your presentation set aside, while something far less satisfactory receives the vote of confidence?

From here on out it need not be so. The techniques of getting ahead are spelled out in the chapters that follow.

Putting yourself and your abilities across consists mostly of skillfully using the key words and phrases that are given. You will learn these words and phrases as easily as you learned your ABC's, and you will be able to use them just as readily. Whatever rung of the ladder you are on, they will help you to solidify your position, to move ahead — with the enthusiastic *help* of your superiors and associates! Naturally, easily, you will put yourself across in every situation — and project the image of a winner — a winner who is liked and admired.

Martha W. Cresci

Contents

**Chapter 2   How You Can Use The Humorous
Phrase To Work Wonders (cont.)**

*Wit in Lieu of a Reprimand 38 • Using Humor to
Relieve Tension 39 • Be Willing to Listen to Troubles 40
• Keys to the Fond Approach 40 • Learn the Humor-
ous Tags of Your Associates 41 • Review This Chapter
Often 43.*

*Temper Criticism With Praise to Get Results 46 • The
Importance of Tact in Managing Others 47 • Take
Care to Temper Harshness 47 • Avoid Gripe Sessions
— How to Do It 48 • Using the Flattering Introduction
to Create Good Will 48 • Phrases that Forestall An-
tagonism 50 • Key Phrases to Use in Differing with a
Superior 51 • Enlisting Aid for Your Viewpoint 52
• Flattering Your Way Out of Hot Water 54 • Avoiding
the Label of "Yes-Man" 55.*

*Attitudes to Avoid in Projecting Your Image 58 • Stick
to the Mores of Your Group to Aid Understanding 59
• Creating an Impression of Openness 60 • Use These
Subjects of Conversation — Be On Guard 60 • How
to Protect Your Secrets Without Seeming To 61
• How to Thaw Out Difficult Personalities 62 • How
to Use Banalities to Avoid Involvement 62 • Don't
Be the Strong, Silent Type 63 • Key Subjects for
Harmless, Productive Conversation 63 • Learn to
Change the Subject for Your Ends 64.*

*The Key Word to Save Being Damaged by Argu-
ments 66 • If You Can't Win, Lose Graciously 67
• The Key to the Successful Technique 67 • Key
Safety Valve Phrases to Practice 68 • Losing
Advantageously 69 • Stature-Building Exit Phrases 70
• How to Give Yourself Another Chance 71 • How to
Win an Argument Gracefully 71 • Managing an Argu-
ment as Chairman 72 • Make Out an Agenda as an*

Chapter 16 **Keeping Your Eye on The Ball —**
For Constant Advancement (cont.)

CHAPTER 1

You Can Talk and Act Your
Way to the Executive Level

Perhaps nowhere more than in business careers is the tremendous power of words demonstrated — the proper use of words, the proper choice of words. As well as controlling the behavior of others, words can control *your own* behavior most effectively and to your benefit. Words can control events, even shape events, and guide the course of action. In the back of our minds most of us know this, yet when we find ourselves in complicated situations we rarely have the time or the detachment to make a studied selection of the words that would be best in a given set-up. Being unprepared, we may be too personally involved, even emotionally involved, and be at the mercy of all cross-currents. One ill-chosen remark may damage an image irreparably.

On the other hand, words can be our servants.

Keep in mind that every minute of every day that you spend in business your first duty is to promote yourself, put yourself across. You do this by doing your work well, of course; but this is not enough for the man who wants to get ahead. In every contact with executives, and with your fellow employees, you must be *selling* yourself. You must make people *notice* the fact that you do your work well, and you must make them like you. You cannot do this selling job overtly, with obvious pushing, striving, and boasting — but do it you must, subtly and surely.

Consider the approaches that must be covered in your daily attitude and in the *speech* that conveys that attitude. Stated positively, these are some of the things you must accomplish:

1. Arouse enthusiastic liking.
2. Make friends.
3. Avoid irritating or angering others.
4. Avoid arousing opposition.
5. Secure the aid and cooperation of co-workers when necessary.
6. Arouse the favorable interest of superiors.
7. Create openings to discuss your ideas.
8. Present ideas and points persuasively.
9. Impress executives with your efficiency and knowledge, yet not arouse jealousy or suspicion.
10. Avoid giving the impression that you are discontented with your present post.
11. Be able to differ without angering others.

The list could be much longer, but these basic points are enough to show how big the job is of putting yourself across.

Herein lies the great value of knowing ahead of time the key words and phrases. Once you know them, you will begin to look at business situations in a new objective way. Careful analysis has shown that all confrontations fall into a fairly limited number of categories, and that each of them can be managed to yield maximum advantage, if one is prepared.

As in a game of cards, the hands that are dealt may be different, but the situations involved can usually be classified. The expert recognizes them quickly and proceeds with the prescribed winning play.

In this chapter we begin at the beginning: how to start your climb. If you are already on the ladder, later chapters will be of increasing interest to you. Nevertheless, you will find this discussion of considerable value. You will doubtless discover some fresh points of view and new approaches to situations everyone encounters in business. Other angles as well as key words and phrases will be gone over. Situations that could have developed into traps will be made opportunities by your new knowledge.

Right here we should point out that there is nothing esoteric about the key words and phrases. They are not special types of words, cabalistic forms like *abracadabra,* with some inherent magic of their own; nor are they two dollar words. On the contrary, the key words are quite simple, ordinary words, for the most part. It is where you use them and how you use them that makes them magical. They are the entrance words, the exit words, the escape words, the temporizing words that turn a situation to your advantage or protect you from damaging embarrassment, even duplicity.

The Attitude Helps Create
the Successful Image

In every business, every human organization, there are always two main groups of people involved. We might label them the initiated and the uninitiated. The uninitiated make up by far the larger group, which consists of those who work each day along one path, staying in one groove, taking orders, collecting their pay. The psychology of most of these is static, and they sometimes act as though they were members of a club, bound forever to its ways and tenets.

They are the underlings, and so wedded are they to their situation that in some organizations they refer to their supeiors and to all executives as "the angels." Well they may, for their own manners and their limited, short-sighted view of things does forever bind them to the lower reaches.

The other group, the initiated, is made up of the executives and leaders, of course. They have a different set of manners, different mores, and an entirely different view of life. They also work, some far harder than the underlings, but they breathe the air of freedom. Their lives are less restricted. For most of them the sky is the limit so far as aspirations are concerned.

Somewhere in between these two groups are a scattered few individuals who feel chained momentarily to the lower group, but who dare to dream and work toward joining the executive echelons. Some of these dreamers make it rather easily. Others never find the keys that open doors to success, in large part because they do not perceive them — perhaps do not even recognize that there are keys.

Starting the Climb

First step on the way upward is to look around you and observe. Study the ways and the manners of the group that you wish to join, then make a plan of action for yourself. Some of the things outlined in this chapter you can begin to do immediately, but major involvements should wait until you have finished the book and learned all the key words and phrases.

You may have the greatest gifts in the world, but if you do not know how to package them properly or present them persuasively, you are likely to remain in the lower ranks. To get ahead, you must learn to "belong," learn how to recognize opportunities and to seize them *gracefully*, how to push yourself *without seeming to,* how to enlist aid rather than arouse opposition. Key words and phrases will be your most important aids, but there are some other factors.

Preparing Yourself for Success

After you have made the decision to try the upward climb, the first step takes place in your frame of mind, believe it or not. It is a matter of "psyching" yourself, and then taking up the other tools of success.

Before you can convince anyone else that you might be executive material, you must thoroughly convince yourself. Sometimes you must change many attitudes, root out latent resentments toward those above you in the organization, and discard any servile posture. Most certainly you must free yourself of the attitudes of the confirmed underlings toward "the angels."

Learning the Earmarks of the Successful

To begin, RELAX! If there is one characteristic that is outstanding among executives in their attitude toward each other, it is that they are relaxed and at ease in each other's company. They have schooled themselves to show no fear, no uneasiness, no apprehension. This relaxed attitude does not mean that manners are abandoned. Quite the opposite. Manners, as a rule, are carefully observed, but as a natural, easy thing.

The same goes for respect. Each person is always given the respect due his office, private opinions notwithstanding. This deference has no taint of servility in it. It is the natural respect of one important person toward another.

There is a key point. If you want to be important, you must feel within yourself that you are important, yet give no hint of pomposity, no manifestation of the braggart.

Now that you are thoroughly relaxed, you can begin to "psyche" yourself. This is something you will do every day, many times a day, until the new attitudes become second nature — indeed, become you. *Start by visualizing yourself as an executive, or at least as executive material.* Some scholars believe that there is a mysterious metaphysical power that assists when you do this. It is more likely that simply by seeing yourself in a certain role, you more or less automatically begin to live and act that role, and to do the things that will help to bring it into reality. Some of these you will do consciously, and others you will do unconsciously. All will have their effect in helping you on your way.

Convince yourself. Believe as you recite your belief.

Use This Model Affirmation to Create Confidence

In addition to visualizing, seeing yourself as an executive, use words. Use the affirmation that follows, or vary it to suit specific needs, but *use words* to sell yourself on your new role. Make the affirmation aloud, if you can do so in privacy, because hearing it as well as thinking it will help to impress your mind with its validity.

- I am executive material. I am respected, and I respect the importance of others.
- I am relaxed and at ease in the presence of executives, because I am one of them.
- I do my job well, because this is my executive responsibility. However,
- I look beyond my job to the big picture.
- The company is important to me.
- Being human, I can err; but I can also admit an error and strive to correct it with the least possible commotion.
- I am an executive, a man of good will and good humor.
- I am an executive. I am on my way up!

Write down your affirmation and memorize it. Go through it many times a day — before every conference, every important contact. Repeat it until your unconscious mind accepts it and your new role is completely natural to you. All else is built upon this basic attitude.

Having made your decision and started to make your new role, you need not abruptly and completely forsake your old companions. Just be careful not to sink back into their psychology and their destructive attitudes. If occasionally they find you distant, do not apologize. Just say, "I have something on my mind." They can understand this.

How to Make Yourself Stand Out

As you begin to ease yourself out of one group, gently ease yourself into the other. Do it by making yourself stand out. Chance encounters are excellent for this. When you meet a superior in the elevator, in a hallway, in a restaurant, never fail to speak. The old weather gambit makes a fine lead-in, but follow it up, connect it with business, if at all possible.

Opening the Way to Spotlighting Yourself

How natural the following openings seem, and yet they set you apart, show that you are interested and alert to the big picture.

Make your own variations where necessary, and use them as an entering wedge to a new association, a way to make yourself stand out as executive-minded.

- Good morning, Mr. Jones. Beautiful day, isn't it? It should really bring the people in for that sale of topcoats.
- (OR) It should speed up work on the Smith construction. Now if it only lasts!
- (OR) It should put our prospects in a good mood! I'm trying to see if I can break the record this month!

Be alert to possible comments you can make on the current business situation. (Give them an optimistic twist, if things have been going badly.) Notice what competitors are doing from day to day. Read the financial pages of the newspaper. Read the trade publications in your field. Know what it is all about, so that you can continue the conversation if the other man gives the go-ahead. Juicy pieces of news or trade gossip are always greeted with interest, as:

- What did you think of J. E. McPherson's leaving Klein and Company?
- (OR) Do you think that J. C. Penny's death will affect their basic policy?

- (OR) I saw in the *Times* that Garrison's are switching to diesels . . .

Sometimes such casual comments bring forth a real triumph, and you are in. In reply to the remark about the diesels, Mr. Jones just might say, "Yes, I had heard some mention that they were considering it, but I had no idea the change would come so soon. Do you know anybody over there? If you do, I wish you'd nose around a bit and see if you can get any information. I wonder if it will pay them on their short runs."

How to Follow Up a Successful Contact

Your answer to this might be, "Well, I don't really know anyone there, but I'll see what I can find out, anyhow." And there you are, with a continuing thread of contact, which, if skillfully handled, can be of immense value to you.

At other times the conversation may just die there, but never mind. It is a beginning, and if Mr. Jones has never bothered speaking to you before, he probably will next time. Just gently and brightly persevere, avoiding any semblance of forwardness.

How to Start a New Job on the Right Foot

On a new job, unless you are already familiar with the organization, some caution is in order. It is important that from the beginning you identify yourself with the "in" group. Until you know who the members are, it is usually best to limit your conversation to pleasant greetings.

In many organizations, there is someone out of favor, perhaps on his way out. Unless you are extremely astute, you may not recognize the situation immediately, and it is astounding what harm can sometimes be done by seeming to be a friend of this person. It will often be assumed that you share his views, that you are against the management, or that at best you are not very discerning. Space yourself this handicap by proceeding warily.

How to Spot the In-Group and Become a Part of It

Oddly enough, it is easier to become a part of the in-group if you are a newcomer than if you are an old-timer in the organization. When you have been around a long time, others' views toward you are congealed. It is possible, however, to make the change. The methods used in both cases are essentially the same. The long term employee, of course, has one advantage, in that he is probably already aware of the members that make up the in-group.

The in-group is the *coterie* that has the management's ear, individually and as a group. One way of spotting them is that they are usually the happiest, most nonchalant group in the place, relaxed and at ease among themselves and with top management.

If you are a lucky newcomer, you will sometimes be introduced to this group immediately. In this case, lose no time in making hay by solidifying your position with this important combination. Without being arrogant or pushy, just assume immediately that you are one of them, and treat them as long-term friends.

Use This Secret of Getting Along With People

One great secret of getting along with people is to forget all shyness, all feeling of strangeness, and to talk to the new acquaintance in the same manner you would use with one of your best friends. This does not mean that you would say exactly the same things to them. Some important secrets can be kept; however, you should give the feeling of openness, warmth, and trust that mark relationships between friends.

This manner, incidentally, is a magic way of making friends anywhere. To use it, you have only to remember that most people are far more alike than they are different; that most human reactions to given events and stimuli are pretty much the same, or at least can be understood by all parties. It is this common bond that makes the majority of people acclaim the same shows, the same books, the world over.

One of the friendliest, most self-confident of the successful men that I have known told me that he had been painfully shy until he learned this truth about common interests. He told me that in the beginning of his career, when he was forced to go to conventions or other gatherings of strangers, he always carried his briefcase with him, or at least some folded sheets of paper. As soon as he entered a crowd of strangers, even at a cocktail party, he would find a table or a shelf somewhere, get out his paper and pencil and start writing! He wrote imaginary reports, his personal budget — anything — so that he would not have to face people.

Occasionally someone would stop and question him about his pretended work. More often, however, he was left alone to suffer. One day, he says, it dawned on him that he simply had to overcome his handicap, if he were ever to get anywhere. He made a mighty resolve, then and there, to start talking to the first person he saw standing alone.

To his amazement, he says, he found that the other man was delighted to have someone to talk to him, although all he had said was, "They've got a nice turnout, haven't they?" Quite soon the two were in a conversation, and were drawing in other people. They went on to enjoy themselves and profit from the meeting.

Of course, the most common way of getting acquainted among strangers is to just stick out your hand and introduce yourself. If you find this difficult in the beginning, just start talking. You do not have to be witty or brilliant. Small talk is perfect. The key is to *require a response* from the other person:

- Make an observation and ask a question to get the other person's view. Show genuine interest.
- Speak in the manner of a friend.
- Keep asking for opinions on inconsequential matters until a conversation is underway.
- *Key Phrases:* "Don't you agree?" "What do you think?" "How do you feel about this?"

More Pointers on Joining the In-Group

Once you have spotted the in-group, make careful mental notes on some of the things that set them apart. If first names are used among them, use first names yourself, casually, unostentatiously.

Note the clothes that are worn. This is often extremely important. In some groups white shirts and conservative business suits are still the uniform. In many others, the sports jacket and more colorful attire in general is the order of the day. Some groups pride themselves in being quite far-out in their choice of clothes. If your appearance makes you stand out as different, make haste to change it, even if you have to secure a loan for the purpose.

Achieving the Successful Look

In choosing your new wardrobe, do not attempt to outshine anyone in the group, in either style or quality — but do have style and quality. If you must skimp anywhere in choosing your outfit, do not skimp on the price or the quality of accessories. In the book, *"What Makes Sammy Run,"* the expensive "sincere" necktie was a symbol of this maxim. Among successful men you will note that neckties, shoes and wallets are always of superior quality, whether the styling be quiet or on the sporty side. Buy the best of these that you can manage. This is not an extravagance, incidentally, as expensive clothes usually last far longer and keep their good appearance to their last days.

Accepting Compliments Gracefully — Key Phrases

If you have chosen your clothes well, they should not attract too much attention; however, you will almost surely receive some compliments. Learn to handle these in a manner that helps you. Whatever you do, never depreciate the article that has been complimented. To imply that the article is not worthy of the compliment is to insult the taste of the person who admired it.

Sometimes a compliment is rather backhanded, implying

that you are trying to outdo others, or that you have too much money to spend on clothes. Never let this annoy you. Remember that the envious person is suffering, so choose a reply that will praise his taste and relieve his feeling of envy, so that it will not develop into dislike or incite competition. Here are some phrases to memorize, so that you will be able to accept a compliment gracefully. Choose the suitable one, or make your own variation. Remember, never insult the taste of the one who gives the compliment. Accept his praise happily, gracefully.

Phrases to Use for Different Situations

- Thanks! I like it, too.
- Thanks! I like it, too. And it's very comfortable.
- Thanks! (Laughing) I ate sack lunches for a month to pay for it!
- Thanks! My father bought it for me for Christmas.
- How about that! I was going through a bunch of sale junk at Wharton's, and I just happened to spot this.
- I'm glad you said that. I like it, but I was sort of wondering if it was too wild. Do you like the side vents? (Or the color . . . or the flap pockets . . .)

Replies like the last one on the list flatter the one who has complimented you by deferring to him as an authority. Therein is another clue to ingratiating yourself and making yourself a part of the group. Last, but not least, do not forget to compliment others on new outfits, and on work well done.

Ask Opinions and Ask for Help if You Want to Be Liked

Do not be a loner. Do not represent yourself as an absolute authority on any subject. You can be informed, you can be educated, skilled, even supremely competent; but you will be wise (and far more likeable) if you admit that there can be other opinions than yours now and then; that there can be areas where help would be appreciated. As a matter of fact, that is an almost sure way to create a warm feeling toward yourself, even in someone who has been rather cool. ASK FOR HELP.

This does not mean, of course, that you should shift your work to others. It merely means that you might ask for a little guidance, perhaps a clarification of policy, or you might ask for an opinion. On rare occasions it might mean the asking of a real favor.

When you do any of these things you are putting your relationship on a warmer, more intimate, more human basis. More important, perhaps, you are indicating unmistakably to the other person that you value his opinion or respect his knowledge and skill. Almost invariably, if you approach him in a friendly but respectful way, he will have a feeling of increased friendliness toward you. These bits of technique even work with a boss that you feel is cool toward you, or overly critical. They are worth trying in any difficult, strained personal relationship.

Some Key Lead-In Phrases

The following are some helpful lead-in phrases. The key words are "I *need* you;" "*Help* me;" "I value *your* opinion." (Do not think you are demeaning yourself in asking others' help now and then. Even the President surrounds himself with advisors and helpers.) Try one of these approaches that fits your situation:

- Bill, I seem to be stymied here for the moment. I wonder if you can help me?
- Mr. Jones, I've gotten to a point on this where I would like your opinion, if you can spare a moment.
- Joe, could you take a few moments to read this over and give me your thoughts on it? I certainly would appreciate it.
- John, I'm not quite clear on what I am supposed to do on this survey. Could you clarify it for me? I would be grateful for your help.

How to Solidify Your Relationships with the In-Group

As soon as possible, work yourself into the social pattern of the organization. Observe who goes on coffee breaks with whom, or to lunch, and ask if you may go along. (It is important to always ask, rather than just tagging along or brazenly seating yourself at the same table.) It helps if you have some contribution to make, in the way of information or a question to be discussed. Study the approaches given below, then write down variations that apply to your field, your situation:

- May I join you fellows? I've got some information on the Brown reorganization that I'd like to tell you about.

- May I come along? I've got an idea that I would like you to give me an opinion on.

- Hey! May I come along? I've got a fantastic joke to tell you!

- Where do you go for lunch? May I join you? I don't know a thing about this neighborhood.

- Will you join me for lunch? If you like seafood, I know of a great place that's not too far.

CHAPTER 2

How You Can Use
The Humorous Phrase
To Work Wonders

Man is a social creature, and he loves to laugh. Whoever helps to introduce a little harmless humor and warmth into the day's business activities is bound to be well-liked—provided, of course, that he does his own job well and does not slow down the works with his levity. The light touch of a bit of banter now and then relieves the deadly routine, and can work wonders. Laughter lets off steam more safely than temper, and the work goes faster.

The bantering, joking relationship is a salient characteristic of the executive group in almost any corporation. It helps greatly to create the feeling of a camaraderie in the executive class. If you have no bent in this direction, study the methods and manners of those who are adept at light humor in your organization before you venture any humor of your own.

Until you feel that you can join in, concentrate on being a good audience. The man who is a good audience is in almost the same honored category as the good listener. Being a good audience, of course, does not mean that you should guffaw at every sally. A chuckle or an appreciative smile is sufficient. Whatever you do, be willing to accept and laugh at a joke that is made at your own expense. To show annoyance or anger is one sure way to make yourself an outcast in short order.

In considering the introduction of humor into your new association, be a little cautious. Be careful not to go overboard. The clown and the buffoon are extremely unwelcome at any level in a business organization. A bit of dry humor, an apt pun, and above all, the light touch in approaching some situations — these are the golden coins that can often gain you much in the executive group. Even they, of course, must be applied with discretion.

How to Use Humor to Create Acceptance, Ease Difficult Situations

The new executive among strangers may find the light touch quite helpful in breaking the ice. Instead of merely introducing yourself to an established employee and letting it go at that, you might say, "I understand you are the man who knows all the answers around here. Could I have a little advice? My name is John Smith."

The response will probably be a pleased laugh and a half-denial, but a conversation will be started, and there will be a basis for the growth of friendship. You will probably also get the needed advice.

Make up your own list of such openings. The following are other good examples:

- "I understand you know all the ropes around here, Sir. I wonder if you could help me undo a few knots? I am John Smith, the new man in Communications."
- "Miss Jones, I am John Smith, the new man in Communications, and I need a friendly guide. I understand you are our expert on policy. Can you give me a steer?"

The light approach and the frank compliment create a pleasant mood in the other person. The real key to success here, of course, is the frank asking for HELP. Any plea for help is almost always honored, unless it is extremely unreasonable. The mere fact that he is asked for help indicates that you consider the person informed and important; and everyone likes to be considered important, be he janitor or senior vice president.

Another time when a touch of humor comes in handy is when you have a job to do that may make you an annoyance to others. Sometimes when you must check and recheck figures, or interrupt someone time and again for reports, you can actually begin to feel like a nuisance. You will be looked upon as one, too, unless you do something about it. An occasional lighthearted introductory remark will put you back into the human being category. Your victim will sympathize with your predicament, rather than considering only his own inconvenience. Even well-worn phrases will do. Try one of the following:

- Here comes that man again!
- Should I throw my hat in first?
- I have some more of those delightful figures for you to check!
- Can you spare another few minutes to your friendly statistician?

To be effective, business humor does not have to be brilliant or original. Strangely enough, people seem to have an affection for the threadbare, homely old sayings. For many people, incapable of originality, these ARE humor. Consider the popularity of such classics as "You can say that again!" and "Join the club!" They have given the average person a satisfactory "witty" reply to be used in many awkward situations. Do not hesitate to use such popular repartee occasionaly if it is current in your group, even if you do it with tongue in cheek. Being too original or too brilliant can sometimes be a social handicap.

If you are a natural wit, of course you will use your powers automatically. One such person that I have known was a detective on the New York police force, and he used his wit quite often to get himself out of a tight spot. Once while he was chauffeuring a police captain through a poor neighborhood he made a right turn too quickly and met head-on a group of boys on skates. As he screeched to a halt, one of the boys had the presence of mind to leap in the air to avoid being hit, and he landed astride the police car's hood. The detective-chauffeur? He stuck his head out the window and yelled, "Get off that car with those skates, boy! You'll scratch the paint!"

The startled boy and the captain exploded into laughter, and the guilty driver was saved a serious reprimand. (Needless to say, no one had been hurt.)

Avoid Using Barbed Wit

Few of us can hope to become as adept as this man at using humor for our own purposes, but we can use it, nevertheless. There are only a handful of important precautions to be emphasized. One of them is to avoid the danger of barbed wit. Never let your sallies degenerate into sarcasm, and avoid making personal jibes that really hurt or that make a person appear ridiculous. In the latter case you will never be forgiven, and only rarely will any benefit accrue.

What is recommended in general for putting yourself across is gentle wit, casual wit, the light touch. You can use it to convey flattery that would be too obvious if said seriously. You can use it to help give a discouraged person new perspective. You can use it to create acceptance in an awkward relationship. You can sometimes even use it as a substitute for a reprimand, especially regarding personal matters.

How to Use Humor to Express Compliments

Most of the people we like and admire are people who like and admire us. If there is someone in the organization whose esteem you want, it is helpful to let him know that you admire him, but this is not always easy to do in a straightforward way. An oblique approach with a touch of humor will often convey the thought. Try a light bit of hyperbole when you greet him, or when you introduce him to another person or to a group. Think of your phrasing ahead of time. Here are a few examples that can be guidelines:

- Good morning, Sir! What's the good word from our chief expert on marketing?

- Good morning, Ma'am! How's our beautiful blonde advertising manager? I think you have done wonders for our image. (Note here that the personal compliment is immediately followed by a reference to business skill, taking away any danger of presumptuous familiarity.)

- Let me introduce you to Bob Myers. He's the real brain in our outfit. (Or) He's our creative genius.

Warm Up a Group with This Technique

Skilled executives often use this same technique to create a warm feeling between themselves and an entire group. I still remember with pleasure an occasion when the president of a company I formerly worked for had called in the advertising staff to hear some suggestions he wished to make. When the copywriters and artists were seated and our immediate director started to seriously explain to us the purpose of the meeting, the president brushed him aside jocularly. "Never mind all that, Clark," he said. "I'll tell these people why I asked them to come here. It's because they are the real brains of the outfit! I want their opinions before we make any changes in our program."

The audience laughed pleasurably, and the skeptical, ruffled attitude with which advertising people characteristically greet the suggestions of "outsiders" was visibly softened. It did not matter that we recognized the ploy. Even sophisticated people cannot help responding in some degree to harmless flattery.

You need not fear being obvious in using such devices. No one cares. The recipient appreciates the feeling of good will behind the effort, and usually responds in a friendly way. He probably thinks, "Well, he must admire us, or he wouldn't say anything so outrageously flattering!"

Easing Corrections and Advice with Humor

A newly hired expert can use similar methods to create a receptive attitude in a group he must address, even though what he has to say may be quite at variance with the introduction. Here is a sample beginning that can be varied to suit the actual situation:

- Coming in here to tell you guys what to do is a little like explaining algebra to Einstein. If you have been told that I am going to do this, forget it. I am actually here to make a study *with you.* I know that each one of you has had plenty of ideas as to what could be done to improve the system, and that is what I am going to depend on. We want to put all these ideas together. (Picks up and sets down pad and pencil.) First I will outline my thoughts off the top of my head, and then I want to hear yours. (Proceeds with speech.)

If the same expert came on with remarks to the effect that he had made a thorough study and found that many of the methods used were wrong and wasteful, his audience would immediately be put on the defensive. He could expect rampant opposition from the word go.

Using Wit in Lieu of a Reprimand

If you cultivate the art of looking for a slightly humorous angle, you can find it useful in countless other situations. Here's an example of its being used to avoid a reprimand of an employee.

In a day when long hair and beards were generally frowned upon, a sales manager I knew used humor to show his disapproval of one man's hirsute appearance.

The man was the last one in for a sales meeting. "Everyone's here but Brown," the sales manager remarked, sitting magisterially at his desk.

"Here he is now," someone announced, as Brown appeared in the doorway.

"Ah, yes," exclaimed the sales manager, seizing a huge pair of paper shears and clicking them dramatically. "Come in, Brown! We're all waiting for you!" Everyone laughed, of course.

"What's the matter?" asked Brown, put on the spot in not too harsh a way. "Don't you like my beard?"

"To tell the truth, I don't," the sales manager replied. "I don't think it helps our image, and it will probably annoy some of your prospects. I'd appreciate it if you would shave it off, before we have to operate on you ourselves."

Such a request is never an easy one to present, but the touch of humor made this one a little less difficult for all concerned.

Using Humor to Relieve Tension

When people are getting too serious or working themselves into discouragement, a bit of humor can also come to the rescue on occasion.

During a business slump a capable merchandise manager was once moaning to me over his declining figures. He looked so woebegone that I thought he needed a little jolt to give him a fresh slant.

"I don't know the answers," he said, riffling dejectedly through the papers before him. "I really don't know the answers."

Just for fun, I gave him a nudge, and in a little girl's voice I piped, "Hmm! I can give you some smart answers!"

"That's what I need! Smart answers!" he exclaimed, but he had to laugh, and his gloomy mood was somewhat dispelled. "Here," he said, rising to leave, "Look over these figures and see what answers you can think of. I'll welcome any suggestions." In other words, he was able to admit now that there might be some solutions to the problems at hand.

As you have probably already learned, there is no use telling a discouraged or depressed person to cheer up, but if you can get him to laugh, you have won half the battle.

You are sitting in your office, and the gloomy, distressed face of a fellow executive looks in your office door. You query, "Hi! What are you looking so perturbed about?"

"Oh, I don't know," the face replies. "Just feeling low, I guess. I thought you might have some solutions."

"Come in, come in," you may say brightly. "I'll let you read my book of business humor!" (Or "play with my yo yo," or "Help me make spitballs . . .")

You may get a boot thrown at your head, but you will almost surely be rewarded with a laugh, and your fellow executive will have some of his gloom dispelled and be better able to see things in proportion. Serious discussion of the problems may follow, but in a more hopeful atmosphere.

Be Willing to Listen to Troubles

The suggestion that you use humor in this manner does not mean that you should brush off another person's troubles or take them lightly. As a matter of fact, after using the humorous invitation, you may follow up with a completely serious question. "What's bothering you?" "What's got you down?" "How is your little son doing?"

After you have asked, listen intently, and make what constructive suggestions you can. Even if you have no solutions to offer, just having you listen will help your friend. (It will often create a friend for you.)

Keys to the Fond Approach

From all the foregoing you can see that humor is a sort of lubricant in business. It eases many difficult situations. It softens and often makes acceptable what otherwise might be harsh. Another important aspect is that it creates warmth and friendly feelings.

If you ever happened to see the dramatization of *The Forsyte Saga* on TV, you will remember the scene where Soames Forsyte was addressing a Board of Directors. In this he gave a splendid example of the dangers inherent in the cold and humorless approach to business. All the other men around the table seemed to have a warm camaraderie, and

Soames was an outsider. It was not because of the difference in rank, since all members respected Soames' ability. It was because he was "all business" and he refused to deal in the little human touches, the bits of humor that bound the others together, in spite of some areas of disagreement. Even when he was right, Soames had extreme difficulty in persuading the other members of the board to listen to his evidence.

This example in reverse illustrates the most important contribution of humor and the light touch in one's approach to business associates. It is absolutely basic to the executive attitude.

You will soon notice when you are among a group of executives that they all express a friendliness toward one another, even a fondness. This holds whether they are associated in the same business or are deadly competitors. A newcomer gets the impression that they are all privy to an "in" joke, or are members of some secret circle. They may depart from this attitude momentarily, when argument gets heated or disagreement flares; but some skillful member of the group will be sure to bring them back to the jolly comrade basis before there is any real damage done. He will usually do it with a touch of fond humor.

Fond. This is a key word in successful business associations. Because they represent that they are *fond* of each other — warmly, indulgently fond — savagery and rudeness rarely erupt among executives. There is an attempt by all parties to keep a warm, friendly attitude, to settle any differences amicably, so that the members can continue to play golf with each other and continue to cooperate in areas where it is to the benefit of all.

If this warm, friendly approach is your natural way with people, you are lucky. If it is not, you must learn it and make it your way, if you hope to succeed. Fortunately, the technique is fairly simple.

Learn the Humorous Tags of Your Associates

It has been my observation that each man is assigned a sort of tag — for the purposes of levity and fun, for a personal angle to the relationship, and as a handy conversation starter. This man may be "the golfer," either a master or a duffer. That man may be the "doting grandparent." Another may be the passionate gardener or the boastful fisherman.

You will soon know which is which, for whenever the group meets these pleasant categorizations become the subject of friendly joshing or interested inquiry. If you are unfamiliar with the person being spotlighted for the moment, be alert to make note of his "tag." Do not hesitate, when necessary, to ask a neighbor at your table to fill you in on the details of how he got the tag. (Of course you will not refer to it as a tag.) Of the golfer, you might say, "Is it true that Burns is a great golfer?"

Your neighbor may laugh and say, "No! He's a terrible duffer, but last Friday he made a hole-in-one by a fluke, and we are never going to hear the last of it."

The speaker will probably finish his story by calling out to the golfer, "Hey Joe! John just asked me if you are a great golfer!" and more merriment will be generated on this subject, until the chairman calls the group to order, or someone asks the fisherman about his latest catch.

As you can see, these handy tags can be used either for friendly joking or for serious conversation. If you happen to share someone's enthusiasm for golf or fishing or gardening, you might want to talk seriously about it for a moment, encouraging a friendship. Be sure you make mental notes or actual notes of the interests of the various group members. The notes will serve you well at future meetings.

When you can greet a person by name it always creates good feeling. If in addition you remember and mention something that is of special interest to him, whether seriously or jokingly, you are on your way to establishing the kind of friendly relationship that is the rule among executives. Unless you are adept at remembering such things, you might keep a little alphabetized notebook in a special shorthand of your own. When you see someone coming, look up his name. He won't know what you are looking up. And who knows, you may soon be kidded about your little black book! Just do not give away its secrets.

Review This Chapter Often

The importance of skillfully used humor in furthering an executive career can scarcely be overemphasized. If you are inclined to be too serious, or if you find your business situation becoming too tense, take time to review this chapter frequently. Each time you read it, resolve to use at least one of the devices described.

CHAPTER 3

How to Use Skillful Flattery
to Ease Difficult Situations

Men have gone to the ends of the earth, literally, seeking admiration and approval. Other men have risked their lives needlessly in battle, or quite deliberately in such foolish and dangerous pursuits as flagpole-sitting — all for the purpose of achieving approval, distinction, or praise. In their excessive hunger for approbation, these men dramatize a need that dwells in every man.

In dealing with those who work for you, give praise whenever you can. We hear stories of slave drivers who belabored their charges with whip and threat. Perhaps there were some, but in every test of productivity, you can be sure that their teams lagged behind those that were praised and encouraged.

Very good! Well done! These are key words that rank with *Please* and *Thank you* in the good executive's lexicon. Use them as often as you can, in one variation or another, and watch the magic that they reap.

Naturally you cannot praise every job that is done, but if you are wise you will check up on yourself at least once a day, to make sure that you have given praise and encouragement wherever possible.

Temper Criticism With Praise to Get Results

Unless a piece of work is outrageously and inexcusably bad, try to find something good to say about it, even when you must criticize it. The basic reasoning here is quite sound. Keep in mind that your purpose as an executive is to get the work done the way you want it, with the least possible friction or delay. If you are impatient and make the mistake of giving bald, untempered criticism, you will not achieve your goal.

Harsh criticism, especially angry criticism, puts a person on the defensive, and usually sets him to thinking of reasons why he is right and you are wrong. He will not be able to listen as well to what you have to say, and he certainly will not work very enthusiastically at making changes. There are even some people, sensitive and intelligent, who cannot function at all under the burden of destructive criticism.

Read over the following phrases and think of times when you might have used them to advantage in the past. This will help you to keep them in mind for future use. If the positive approach to criticism is new to you, memorize the phrases, adding some variations of your own; then use one of them the next time an occasion arises. When you do so, note how well the soft technique works in easing a difficult situation. Here are a few suggestions:

- In the main, this is very good, Jones, but there are a few points you haven't covered. I am sure you can work them in.
- This is certainly a neat way of presenting the material, Miss Smith, but unfortunately you have given me the Klein figures instead of the Haynes. You had better drop everything and see how quickly you can get the Haynes figures organized.

- I am sure you have a good reason for arranging the stock this way, Garrison; but it simply won't work in with our particular system. Let me explain why.

- I don't know what happened here, Kent. You are usually excellent at putting these ideas across, but I think you have missed the main point this time. You'd better go down and have a cup of coffee, and then make a fresh start. You might refer back to that James thing you did that was so good.

(Or) Perhaps I didn't make clear what was wanted. Here is a sample that you might use as a model.

The Importance of Tact in Managing Others

In some of the cases cited above, you may feel that you are flattering the blunderer, and indeed you may be; but you are doing so for a good and positive purpose. Discriminating flattery in such instances is just one of the useful tools that come under the heading of TACT.

Webster defines *Tact* as *a fine sense of how to avoid giving offense.* Think about that. Whether you are at the top or on your way up, no single quality is more important than tact in the art of putting yourself across. Combine tact with creativity, suitable aggressiveness, the knowledge and skills needed in your field, and you will just about have it made. Without this one quality, for instance, managerial ability is nonexistent.

The tactful approach requires that you look at every person as a human being, whether he is above you or beneath you. It requires that you take into account his feelings, his pride, his need to preserve his sense of importance. We might note here that even the most boastful and seemingly conceited person has these needs. As a matter of fact, his boasting is done more to convince himself than to convince other of his prowess. The boaster is practically pleading with you to help bolster his ego!

Take Care to Temper Harshness

The use of tact in dealing with subordinates, as we have demonstrated, is a fairly simple matter. It requires mainly that you take care to temper harshness. The use of tact in dealing with superiors is certainly equally important. Here, outright compliments, even flattery, if skillfully done, can be of value to the ambitious executive. In the latter case there are many more occasions when this harmless softening influence might be helpful; but naturally you must guard against becoming too obvious.

It goes without saying that there should be a background of sincerity in your complimentary approach — and of consistency. If you compliment your superior to his face, you cannot very well join in secret gripe sessions where his image is torn apart. To do so would not only be reprehensible, but could lay you open to devastating attack by your associates.

Avoid Gripe Sessions — How to Do It

For the purposes of your own advancement, you would do well to avoid the dangerous gripe sessions in any case. You might be wise to brush them off with an impatient, "Oh you guys! Can't we talk about something else?" There is nothing to be gained from such discussions, and they always leave a residue of bitterness which may carry over into your behavior for hours or days afterward. If you feel that you must unburden yourself, your trusted spouse is about the only person to whom you can safely bring such talk.

The so-called "Encounter Sessions" that burgeoned on every hand at one period have attempted to counteract this view in favor of complete frankness in all relationships. It might be pointed out here that psychologists are not businessmen, and that over the centuries the devices of courtesy and pleasant circumspection have proved their value in business activities. It is impossible to love everyone, but, by and large, we can learn to be polite to everyone.

Using the Flattering Introduction
to Create Good Will

In regard to anyone whose good will you wish to cultivate, introductions present a wonderful opportunity. Whether you are introducing your superior to an individual or a group

. . . a business acquaintance, a friend, your wife, or the company at a banquet . . . use the occasion to let him know your good opinion of him. Formulate in your mind ahead of time some appropriate phrases to use, so that you will be ready.

You have heard it hundreds of times, and nothing sounds more stupid or is more of a conversation-stopper than the standard introduction: *I'd like to introduce you to my boss.* When your turn comes, give it a little interest, a little zip. You will accomplish many good purposes besides making him feel important and more favorable toward you. For one thing, the fact that you work for such a capable man will make you seem more important. For another, it will lend prestige to the business establishment you both work for. Last, but not least, the complimentary introduction tells the other party something about the man you are introducing, and immediately suggests questions or comments that will open a conversation. Such information is definitely part of a gracious introduction anywhere.

In formulating your own introduction phrases, consider these as models:

- I would like to introduce you to the head of our company, John Jones. He designed our new city hall, as you'll probably remember. Mr. Jones, Bob Smith, a friend of mine.
- Mr. Jones, I would like to present my friend, Elliot Bacon. Mr. Jones is my boss, and he is just about the greatest merchant I have ever known.
- Mr. Jones is my boss. He was just explaining to me the principle behind fluid computers. If you have any question about computers, he is the man who knows the answers.

A word here about the order of names in an introduction might be helpful to you if you are not familiar with it. Just remember that you present the less important person to the more important person — as you present a commoner to the

Queen. However you phrase it, this is the basic structure behind the proper introduction. Thus you present a man to a lady, a younger person to an older person, and a friend to the boss, if you want to be meticulously correct. Many people consider this important; however, if your introduction is flatteringly and pleasantly phrased, no one is likely to notice the order. A conversation will begin too quickly!

This is as good a place as any for a tip on your own manners when you are introduced to someone (not everyone knows these rules). Men always rise when being introduced, whether to a man or a woman (ladies do not). A man always shakes hands with another man when they are introduced. A man never shakes hands with a lady, UNLESS she offers her hand. A glove need not be removed for handshaking, if it is hard to remove. And, for heaven's sake, never say, "Pardon my glove!" Say instead, "Excuse me for not removing my glove."

Remember always, however, that people will forgive any little oversight or slip if you are a pleasant enough fellow. Do not allow yourself to become embarrassed and confused if you make an error. Just ignore it and go on with the conversation.

Phrases that Forestall Antagonism

One of the most difficult situations in business for anyone is the occasion when you must differ with one in authority, even point out to him that he is wrong. Many men who think of themselves as executives simply avoid this problem by ignoring it. They never differ! Perhaps some of them hope that someone else will accept the burden of telling the boss that he is wrong. In such a case, they occasionally lend their support to the front man. On the other hand, if no brave champion arises, the error is just permitted to continue, regardless of what it does to the business.

This is not only a cowardly attitude, but a foolhardy one, from every point of view. Errors of judgment on the part of leadership are costly, and what is bad for the business is bad for the individuals who depend on it for their livelihood. This is basic. It is also basic that if you adopt a policy of never expressing disagreement, you become a colorless, rubber-stamp personality. Even the most authoritarian of business leaders, if they are intelligent, come to recognize such figures in their retinue, and are loathe to promote them to positions of any real responsibility.

It is much better to plan ahead, to be prepared for what you will do, what you will say, when it becomes necessary to point out your superior's error to him. Here tact and gentle flattery can be tremendous allies in preserving a good relationship between yourself and the man you work for. The idea is to get your point across and have it accepted, without humiliating your important adversary or setting yourself up as being more capable than he is. Never mind getting "credit" for the correct idea or procedure. You may have to wait for long term gains in this respect, in favor of preserving your present good relationship and continuing your usefulness to the company.

Remember that in this situation, as in many others you will encounter, your complimentary or apologetic lead-in does not necessarily have to apply to everything that follows in your remarks. In many cases the lead-in is only seemingly relevant, and is just a tool to keep from wounding feelings and arousing antagonism. People do not always remember exactly what you said a few minutes before, and they do not demand that all parts of a conversation be cohesive. They only observe that you are a pleasant, likable fellow, with a good head on your shoulders!

Key Phrases to Use in Differing with a Superior

Study and memorize some of the introductory phrases used in the following examples of differing with a superior. You will find them useful in many difficult situations.

- There is no one whose opinion I respect more than yours in this field, Mr. Blank, but there is an angle which occurs to me that I think we should discuss.
- I know you are a recognized authority in this field, Sir.

I wish you would consider this point a moment and let me know your thoughts.

I agree with you that we should pamper our old customers, but it seems to me that the younger generation that is coming up is different from anything we have dealt with in the past. I believe it is important to study this market and perhaps develop new techniques.

- There is certainly much merit in what you have said, Mr. Green. I agree that we should put most of our emphasis on the eastern markets because of the freight differential. However, I was reading an interesting thing the other day. I wonder if you would discuss it a moment.

- I particularly liked your point about economy. I think there is a lot of fat that we can pare off. I hope, though, that in doing so we can find a little funding for continuing the A Department Research. Perhaps if we want to do it badly enough we can find the money in other economies. (Here you lead in with one point on which you do agree and gently introduce an area of disagreement in a tentative way.)

These same introductions or variations of them can sometimes be used when your idea has been suppressed and you think it is important enough that it should be revived for further discussion. You throw your opponent off-guard for a moment with seeming agreement, and as he goes into a recapitulation of his own thoughts you can sometimes present your own viewpoint a second or third time.

Enlisting Aid for Your Viewpoint

On occasion, when you believe that your boss is absolutely wrong in his approach to a situation, he may be adamant. Here you can sometimes use a touch of flattery to enlist the aid of your fellow executives. The technique is to drop the subject with your opponent momentarily until you can do a little behind-the-scenes investigation.

In one smaller company in which I worked, all the executives used this method in order to keep the company afloat. The man we worked for was given to wild ventures, and was mesmerized by what he considered the glamour and drama of certain escapades. Even when he had lost $50,000 on a similar tack, he would sometimes endeavor to try it again. Short of tying him up and holding him down, there was nothing we could do to save him and ourselves except to consolidate our opposition by tactful maneuvering in the background. Many times our secretly organized counter-arguments prevailed, when all seemed lost in the first skirmish.

In such vital situations a little flattery will often persuade colleagues — even the timid fellows and the yes-men — to back you up. The approach is simple, and phrased in such a way that it cannot be criticized. Here are a few lead-ins to keep handy in the back of your mind:

- Bill, you're a level-headed guy. I'd like to ask your opinion on something. With the market situation the way it is, do you really think it's wise for us to call in those bonds now? I'm worried about it.
- Jim, I'm worried about something, and I'd like to have your opinion on it.
- Karl, I have a high regard for your knowledge on these things. I wonder if you could explain Mr. Brewster's thinking to me on this A-G merger? Frankly, I'm concerned about it.

After the lead-in, and after the opinion or explanation is given, you go into your own thoughts and fears on the matter. In summing up, and after having persuaded your colleague, you might say: Well, thanks, Bill, for giving me your thoughts. I think the matter is so important that I am going to bring it up again and really have it out with Mr. Brewster. I hope you'll back me up, if he asks you about it. We should at least make him consider all the angles.

Note the persuasive use of "we" in the last sentence; and note the accent on your worry and concern for the company in the suggested lead-ins.

Flattering Your Way Out of Hot Water

So far what we have discussed on the subject of flattery and tact might be classed as the aggressive uses, or the positive uses. Variations of these techniques can also be extremely useful when you happen to find yourself on the defensive.

Take a situation in which you are being criticized by a superior, when he is impatient with you, or taking you to task. It is rarely helpful to your cause if you meet the accusation or criticism head on, or with an angry response. The old Biblical admonition to agree with thine adversary quickly is surprisingly more effective. You avoid an argument that could be disastrous, you mollify your antagonist, and you give yourself another chance or more time, in many cases.

Prepare yourself now to handle any such situation skillfully, if it should ever arise. Being ready will almost surely keep you from the fatal error of losing your temper, and will give you command of the situation. The best answer is the tactful one, and often the flattering one. Here are some good examples to adopt:

- I can see why it appears that way, Sir, and I don't blame you for being annoyed. But the fact is that there has been a delay in materials arriving . . .

- Sir, I know you could do this much faster than I can at present. I've had to sort of feel my way; but I am sure I've got it now and I am picking up speed.

- Well, I am up against a problem, Sir. I wonder if you could give me some pointers. I know you are a past master at handling such things.

- I agree, Sir. I made a mistake. But I think I have everything in hand now. I wish you would go over it with me, and give me your expert opinion.

- I agree, Sir. I made a mistake, and I won't do the same thing again. I am looking forward to the day when I am as skillful at this sort of thing as you are. You can be sure I'm trying.

It must be said here that the soft answer, even the flattering answer, does not work 100 percent of the time in turning away wrath. There are a few characters in business who tend to mistake courtesy and reasonableness for cowardice. With these the soft answer just invites further attack. In such rare confrontations you will have to let your own anger, or simulated anger, lash out. When you do so, do so because it is necessary; be careful not to really lose your temper. Let your words be spontaneous, yet carefully chosen.

Avoiding the Label of "Yes-Man"

An additional caution should perhaps be emphasized again, before we leave this subject. In using a tool like flattery to put yourself across, it is important not to overdo it. Gratuitous, bald flattery that has no real purpose, except to ingratiate, can soon become rather obvious. As applied to your superiors, save this valuable aid for the times when you really need it, or when it is very apropos. If you are at all doubtful about your ability to judge these occasions, re-read this chapter. The man who gives a sincere compliment now and then is respected and appreciated. The one-man claque and the fawning yes-man are rarely very successful beyond a certain level.

CHAPTER 4

How to Use the Banal
to Solve Problem Situations

"Be sweet, dear maid, be sweet, and let who will, be clever."

Before the turn of the century, this was the maxim that anxious mothers tried desperately to engrave in the hearts of their female offspring.

Quaint? Yes. And yet, if we crossed out *dear maid* and substituted *ambitious man or woman,* it might not be a bad slogan for aspirants to live by in modern business. All of which is to say that intellectual wit and cleverness are no asset to the process of getting ahead. If you lack them, do not give it a thought. If you have them, suppress them, at least for eight hours a day! The possessor who parades these qualities is suspect. The apprehensions and the sense of inferiority he engenders in others do not breed trust and congeniality.

Friendships and the inspiring of trust, of course, are prime ingredients of the successful career, and the need cannot be overstressed. In many businesses "report cards" or "evaluations" of executives are kept in their individual files, to be referred to when promotions are being considered. Above all, these evaluations stress the ability to get along with other people — subordinates, equals, and superiors. This ability to get along with people, to make friends, is often considered more important than actual job knowledge.

In order to make friends, of course, you must make people like you; you must fit in with the group. You must be able to talk with anyone on a friendly level. It is here that banalities often serve a useful purpose.

Attitudes to Avoid in
Projecting Your Image

Humor and the light touch in your daily relationships is important, as has been discussed in Chapter Two, but the humor is the broad, simple type that is universally understood. This simple humor actually greases the wheels of business and makes them run more smoothly. On the other hand, pungent wit, salty or morbid humor, and extreme cleverness with intellectual overtones, are types distinctly to be avoided. Our civilization, and especially our business structure, worships the wholesome norm. Brains, supposedly, are at a premium; but the brains that are wanted are the sensible, properly directed kind.

Just as you should strive to make your clothes fit the fashions of the "in" group in your organization, so should you tailor your conversational style and your general outlook. In most groups you can rarely say anything too dull; but you can be too clever a conversationalist for your own good, too learned in the classics, too fond of strange two-dollar words. Any of these may stamp you as an intellectual, and the intellectual is not often accepted as good executive material. The sound basis for this, again, is that such a person is not generally understood, and people have the feeling that his thoughts go beyond them. They will probably suspect that he may not have all the respect he should for the solid old American virtues, or even for business principles.

Stick to the Mores of Your Group
to Aid Understanding

A man I know once put up a motto in his office that read, "Think small. Big thoughts scare people." This struck him as very funny because it illuminated some of his defeats; his boss, however, was infuriated by the sign. The superior took it as a personal insult and an important relationship was damaged, perhaps irreparably. For the small pleasure it gives you, do not allow yourself the luxury of such sardonic humor within business confines. Stick to the tried and true, the mores of your group.

Acceptable conversation, even at luncheons and quasi-social affairs, is more or less strictly limited to business and business personalities. The center of attention is the man who has wide knowledge of different business outfits in his field, and the personalities involved. The first man with a piece of juicy gossip or advance news of mergers and other business changes is eagerly listened to. Read your trade publications religiously for background material. Discussion of what is going on in the field and thoughts on the effects it may have on your own organization are the earmarks of top executives.

In business discussions you can use as many technical and high-powered words as you wish, if they are related to your field and are understood. In this connection you will note the importance of fashionable words, and how they are savored by the in-group. At one period everything may be tagged as "relative" or "not relative." "Parameters," you may have noticed, was a pet word of the elite at one time.

In another period, "germane" may supersede "relative," and "extrapolation" crowd out "parameters." Keep your ears alert to these changing vogues, and rush to your dictionary privately when necessary. When you look up the "new" words, practice their use by writing down the definition, and then writing three or four sentences that apply the words to some situation in your own line of work. Because these words are fashionable and are applied to your own business, they do not carry the burden of intellectuality. They will enhance your image, but their use should be reserved for important discussions and they should not be over-used. They should not be used where they will not be understood.

Creating an Impression of Openness

If you have been having some difficulty in getting your personality across or in cementing warm business relationships, think over some of your conversations and some of the occasions when your talk fell flat. You may find the reasons in your choice of subject or your choice of words. In the future make it a point to stick to business and business personalities, and to small talk as much as possible. Feel your way.

Trust and friendliness — remember, these are what you are trying to establish between yourself and business associates. You can only do it on the basis of *their* values, if yours are different. Herein lies one of the failings of our schools, and of some otherwise intelligent parents. In college one may have great admiration for a scholarly professor and his brilliant academic approach. He may teach you to actually poke fun at business and businessmen. If you accept this teaching you may be in for trouble, since business is to be your occupation. It is better to look upon such opinions as just one point of view, emanating from an ivory tower. Sinclair Lewis would have been an abject failure in business!

Use These Subjects for Conversation —
Be On Guard

There is really no great difficulty in finding material for enjoyable personal conversations with business associates. There are certain common denominators among the experiences of people, no matter what their life style, and these make excellent grist for establishing warm relationships. A great mass of material can be used to create an impression of openness and humaneness, and yet not give away too much of your personal life.

It is a mistake, as a rule, to share really personal features of your life with others. If you do not get along with your wife, keep it to yourself. This is such a sensitive area in everyone's experience that you can never know what judgments are being made of *you* as you criticize your spouse. If you are taken off guard with a personal question in this direction, as occasionally happens, be ready with a pleasant, noncommittal reply, such as, "Oh, we have our differences now and then, but most of the time we get along fine. She's a great gal!"

How to Protect Your Secrets
Without Seeming to

The same thing goes for your children. If you are having real trouble with them, are perhaps involved with juvenile authorities, do not reveal it and let it become a subject of whispers and gossip. Protect your children and yourself. Once again, serious trouble with your children may reflect unfavorably on you. Justly or not, people are bound to wonder why you cannot manage your own children.

I once knew a personnel manager who was ruined because he confided a "secret" to one friend. It spread like wildfire in a 5000-man organization, and all respect for the executive departed. The only thing that people could think of or discuss among themselves, when they saw him, was the disgrace of his daughter. He had always been a rather finicky man, too critical of others, and the enemies he had made now had a field day destroying his image.

Note that this prohibition on talk of children applies only to *serious* trouble with your youngsters. One of the great bonds between mature people is their outrage, or pretended outrage, at the foibles of the younger generation — when these foibles are comparatively harmless. Another parent who is complaining about the way his son cuts his hair, or the state of his teenage daughter's room, will love you if you chime in with some humorous comment about your own offspring's failings in similar directions. It relieves the other parent's feeling of inadequacy when you in effect tell him that all parents go through the same things. You will probably get him to laugh about the situation, which will do you both good.

These examples demonstrate the fine line that divides suitable and unsuitable talk on a personal level, insofar as it serves you or does you a disservice. A certain amount of *carefully selected* personal talk is very useful in creating friendliness in others.

How to Thaw Out Difficult Personalities

Take the case of a business associate whom you see frequently but who continues to keep you at a distance, maintains a cold and "businesslike" attitude. This is not good. It is important to make a friend of such a person. Among other things, it will help you to know his personality and to judge what he is thinking. It will also make your contacts more pleasant for both of you. Try softening up the cold type with a little genuine, personal interest on your part.

If he looks tired, seems nervous or irritable, you can often make things easier for him and begin a friendlier relationship by showing him that you think of him as a person. A simple, "You look tired today. What's been happening?" will sometimes make him physically jump. It is as though he said, "I didn't realize you cared!" And the first thing you know, he will be telling you, briefly or at some length, what it is that is troubling him.

All people are lonely to some extent, and tend to feel isolated in a cold world. A touch of well-meaning interest and a bit of reassurance are received gratefully, even if you only say, "Well, don't let it get you down. You'll have it organized soon." Try it.

How to Use Banalities to Avoid Involvement

There are numerous such situations in which a rather meaningless banality serves a useful purpose. For instance, in listening to others' troubles you sometimes do not really wish to get involved, because the subject is too delicate, too fraught with danger. Yet you do not wish to seem unsympathetic or unconcerned. Here the old tried and true cliches, like the above, can be useful. Others include, "Well, you know what they say. You can't fight city hall!"

As you are leaving your new confidant, be sure to say, "Let me know what happens," to assure him of your continuing interest. And the next time you see him, make a mental note to ask him how everything turned out. Doubtless he will be your friend from now on. Another word of caution, however. Be sure not to repeat the stories related to you unless you are told that you may, or you find that the tales are a subject of general knowledge.

Don't Be the Strong, Silent Type

Just as you yourself may have worried about the man described above, who never made a friendly gesture, others may worry about you if you are too reserved. The childish literature that extolled the virtues of "the strong, silent type" surely did a great deal of harm to young people who sought to emulate such "heroes." The sophisticated among us would call these heroes inhibited, frustrated, fearful — perhaps "warped personalities" — and speculate about the faults in their upbringing and their love life. The less analytical would simply tag one of these characters as unfriendly, or "a cold fish." Neither assessment can do a man any good.

Never let yourself lapse into a so-called strong, silent image, whether it is with superiors or with those who work for you. This is not to say that you must be the jolly, back-slapping extrovert every minute. It only means that you should take time to be *friendly,* with all that the word implies.

Key Subjects for Harmless, Productive Conversation

Here are subjects you can discuss with anyone, no matter what the footing. Banal? Perhaps so, but they can make up an important part of the technique of getting along with people. If you have any difficulty at all in thinking of things to talk about, check over the list and write down several topics for later use. All of these have a slightly personal quality.

- His game or his hobby.
- His new car or the old beat-up car he clings to.
- Traffic tickets.
- His trip.
- His son or daughter.
- His new grandchild.
- His opinion on restaurants, movies, etc.

Learn to Change the Subject for Your Ends

While we are on the topic of conversation, it is important to take up the matter of evading discussions you wish to avoid or to nip in the bud. On such occasions, as when someone asks a personal question or two associates are perhaps treading on dangerous territory, do not hesitate to interrupt; but do it adroitly. Think of a joke you must tell, or a bit of gossip. Compliment someone's outfit, or a job well done.

Muster a tone of excitement, and say, "Before you go on with this, fellows, let me tell you some news I heard!"

When you have finished your story the whole trend of the conversation may change, and the delicate subject be forgotten. If it is not, you can excuse yourself on urgent business and make your exit. In the case of the personal question, simply say, "I'll have to talk to you about that later. I just remembered I am supposed to be in J. D.'s office this minute." Or perhaps, "I was supposed to meet my wife at Childs'." No one has any real right to ask personal questions, and you have every right to evade them — but do so inconspicuously.

CHAPTER 5

How to Win—or Lose—
an Argument Advantageously

"You're wrong! It can't possibly work! I'll stake my reputation on it!" Words like these sound like dialog from an old play. Yet business arguments do occasionally become so heated that emotions take over, and an otherwise competent executive may forget his personal objectives and utter such words. If he thereupon loses the argument, he probably stamps out of the arena in fury — creating a personal tragedy.

For a moment of childish abandon, such a man has not only lost face in losing the argument but he has damaged himself immeasurably, almost certainly endangered his future. Moreover, if he does not backtrack immediately with an apology, he may even have endangered his job.

We must, it is true, put our hearts into what we are doing, if there is to be any success or any pleasure in business; and yet it is vitally important never to forget the proper techniques. The proper techniques are the techniques of *accomplishment*. These make everything work *for* you — even the losing of an argument.

The Key Word to Save Being
Damaged by Arguments

There is a key word to keep in mind during arguments, whether your side is winning or losing. Perhaps we should call it a watchword, rather than a key word, because it is a word not to speak, but to live by. The word is *MAG-NANIMITY*. Of all the qualities in the makeup of the successful man, one of the most important is certainly this one — *MAGNANIMITY*. Look it up in the dictionary, even if you think you already know its meaning. Write it down and think about it. The word has to do with bigness, and it is a quality of big men.

The man quoted above forgot to be magnanimous; and you may also forget unless you fix the need of it firmly in your mind. The danger lies in the fact that the type of man who is reaching for the top is practically always an aggressive, hard-driving personality with a certain single-mindedness. If he thoughtlessly follows his natural emotional bent, he may drive himself right into a corner on more than one occasion. Be wary of this danger, and resolve now to make arguments and debates work in your interest, whether you win or lose them.

Remember, the two sides of an argument, winning and losing, both present dangers *and* opportunities in regard to your image and your career, regardless of the substance of the argument.

The subject of the argument may be extremely important to the business, but it is not particularly important to you personally, unless you handle yourself badly in regard to it. Because it is important to the business, or seems so at the time, you must give it your serious attention, and present your viewpoint completely. Yet you must not get so carried away that you lose sight of your own personal objective.

And what is your objective? It is to present yourself always as the competent executive, in control of the situation and in full control of yourself. You must be an embodiment of wisdom and dedication, where arguments are concerned, and not a passionate partisan. Although you are a participant, you must behave as a judge, weighing the facts as you and others present them.

Even if you feel strongly about one side or the other, you will not hurt your case by assuming this judicial attitude. You will grow in stature, and what you say will be enhanced, carry more weight. By the same token, your own judgment will be improved by the lack of emotionalism.

If You Can't Win, Lose Graciously

There is one big point to be made about losing, and that is that if you must lose, lose graciously. If you are positively going to have to do something you do not approve of or that you disagree with, the fact is that you are still going to have to do it. There is certainly nothing to be gained by fuming about it or even pouting about it — within the confines of the business establishment, at least. (If you must blow off steam, reserve the display for your understanding spouse, where no harm can be done.)

Let us go back to the man we discussed at the beginning of this chapter. Just reading his words, when they do not apply to anything at all, arouses a feeling of anger and opposition in the reader. This is what makes them so bad. The words are a challenge to a contest, not in any way conducive to a search for the truth. In using them he is making an egotistical spectacle of himself, and is not gaining one whit for his side of the discussion.

The Key to the Successful Technique

The key to the successful technique is the remarkable fact that anything you want to say can be said courteously; and it becomes, if anything, more effective. Let us examine the words of the angry man, and some mature alternatives to his phrasing:

- (Self-damaging) You are wrong. (Beneficial) I can't quite go along with your thinking, Bob. It seems to me there are certain insurmountable obstacles. Take the matter of deliveries. We are just not equipped to handle this perishable material, and I doubt if we want to go to the expense of getting refrigerated trucks. What do you say about that angle?

- (Self-damaging) It can't possibly work.
  (Beneficial) I can see your point in wanting to do this, but I just don't believe it is feasible. I'd like to tell you why I think this.

- (Self-damaging) I'll stake my reputation on it.
  (Beneficial) Before we make a final decision on this, let me outline for you some of the experiences others have had with this sort of diversification. Take Brown & Company in St. Louis . . .

Studying the acceptable alternatives, you will note that they are all pedestrian and thoughtful in their wording, calculated to soothe tempers and inject reason. They also give due respect to the opponents' motives and thinking abilities. They are magnanimous, mature. They show concern for the business rather than for personal victory. Even in reading them over, you become ready to listen to this thoughtful, careful man.

Key Safety Valve Phrases to Practice

This controlled, judicial attitude toward arguments is particularly difficult for some personalities to adopt, and yet it is only common sense. If you are the impulsive type, with a tendency to blurt right out when you object to what is being said, there is an extra safeguard you can employ. There are certain rather meaningless temporizing phrases that serve two purposes in incendiary situations. They effectively halt proceedings, signaling that you wish to speak; and they forestall any ill-chosen rejoinders on your part.

Practice these phrases in private, visualizing situations in which they might be useful. Here are a few such safety valve phrases that will halt your adversary momentarily without offending him, and will give you a moment in which to properly phrase your objections:

- *Let's stop right here for a minute!* I believe the rest of us might have some ideas on this that could be of value.
- *Hold on a minute!* An idea just came to me.
- *That sounds intriguing, Bob, but let's put it on the table for a moment and examine it.*
- *You've opened up a big question there.* Let's talk about it a bit.
- *That's an interesting angle, I must say,* Bob; but hold on a minute. Let's examine it.

A good way to learn more such phrases and the useful techniques that go with them is to watch some of the better talk shows on TV. On those shows where eminent personages are being interviewed, you can watch and listen to some of the masters. The *William F. Buckley* program is a good example, as is *Meet the Press,* and some others. Without cost you may have Presidential aspirants and even the Secretary of State as teachers!

Losing Advantageously

Temporizing, taking a judicial attitude — these are the techniques for proceeding with an argument. But what about an out and out loss of an argument, when all that you have believed in concerning the question is put down? What do you do then?

The answer is quite simple. You bury the hatchet and concede defeat with *magnanimity,* somewhat in the spirit of a prizefighter rushing forward to congratulate the man who beat him. You, of course, will not bear any visible scars from the encounter, because you have taken care to see that the argument has not degenerated into a personal encounter. *You are not a defeated champion, but a wise judge* who accepts the jury's verdict!

In choosing the remark you will use to concede defeat, you do not have to make a big thing of it or act as though your opponent has achieved a tremendous victory. Your object is to present yourself as a reasonable man who has been persuaded. If possible, you will try to show by inference that you really have no personal feeling about the matter. You will also indicate that you are a member of the team, willing to give all cooperation in pursuing the chosen course.

Stature-Building Exit Phrases

Arguments and debates in business have varying degrees of importance to the organization. Choose an exit phrase that is suitable to the subject discussed. Conceding defeat on the approval of a merger, for instance, would require a different choice from a matter like the proposed color of a new label. Following are several suggestions. Memorize a few for possible later use.

- After considering all the angles, I am now inclined to agree with Bob.
- Well, you have persuaded me. I take back my objections. I believe we can handle them.
- I'll go along with the majority. I don't believe the drawbacks are insurmountable. We can make it work.
- Well, you gentlemen have certainly made a good case. I will support it 100 percent. You can count on my full cooperation.

In weighty matters it is especially important to stress your complete willingness to cooperate. You need not overdo this, but make it completely clear that you will not let lingering doubts interfere with promoting the success of the project. This is another case where, if you must do something, you should do it graciously. You can only harm yourself by expressing reservations, or worse yet, taking a sorehead attitude. You can be sure that if the project does not turn out well, and the final decision proves to have been unwise, everyone will remember your having opposed it — whether all admit it or not. In this situation you do not want anyone to have the feeling that you might have sabotaged the project or given it less than your full, active support.

On the other hand, if the project decided upon does succeed or prove to be a wise choice, you are in the clear, as a *participant in the decision.* You can emphasize this generously, by saying, "I must admit that you men were right in making this decision. I had a few misgivings there for a while, but I don't have any now!"

How to Give Yourself Another Chance

There are occasions like those we have discussed in which you cannot in all conscience agree offhandedly. In these cases try to defer action, if at all possible. The following phrases and techniques are helpful:

- Why don't we delay a decision on this until all of us can give it a little more study? There is so much difference of opinion, I would like to suggest that we adjourn and meet again Wednesday.
- I should like to hear Bill Brown's thoughts on this. He has had much experience in the field. Can't we wait until he gets back?
- I think the engineering department ought to be in on this decision. Can we get them in? Maybe we could meet with them tomorrow?

Of course, if you fail in this maneuver, there will be nothing for you to do but go along with the majority. If you still believe that you must cling to your opposition — and to do so is usually unwise — do it in a positive way. You might say, "Well, I still have some doubts, but I will cooperate with you fellows 100 percent. I will do everything I can to make it work. Where shall we begin?"

How to Win an Argument Gracefully

If you happen to be the winner in a hard-fought argument, you might think, at first blush, that you will be in clover. Such is rarely the case. In an emotionally charged situation you can very easily get yourself into the position of winning the battle and losing the war. Here again *magnanimity* is the key to success.

You, yourself, may have maintained the proper judicial attitude during the discussion, but others may have allowed too much feeling to enter into their side of it. Without being obvious, it is your job now to soothe them, and to assure that they will cooperate willingly in the course that has been chosen. You must help your opponents to save face.

Avoid like the plague any crowing attitude, any semblance of triumph. Unless you are forced to comment, the best thing to do is probably to do nothing. Do not emphasize your success in any way, unless it is necessary; just go on to the next question on the agenda.

In other situations you may be forced to comment, as in a case where you are the person who must implement the decision. Perhaps you must even look for assistance among those who have opposed you heatedly. It is here that magnanimity can again be your ally. Phrases like the following may help to achieve harmony and dissipate any hard feelings against you:

- There was a lot of sense in what you said, John; but I believe we have made the right decision. I'll certainly need your skills in carrying this out.
- I hope you don't think there was anything personal in my opposing you, Fred. You know I always have the greatest respect for your opinions. I will want you to help me outline the new project.
- See me after the meeting, will you, Don? I would like you to help me draw up the plan.

Asking for help, when it is possible, restores a sense of stature to those who may have felt downgraded. Note the use of first names. If you have ever called these men by their first names, do so now. It adds warmth, even an affectionate quality, to your remarks.

Managing an Argument as Chairman

Occasionally in business you will be called upon to chair a group in which an argument is rampant, and this position also calls for skillful techniques. If the meeting is conducted according to Roberts' Rules of Order, problems are minimized. It is the informal meeting that can present real problems to the chairman.

Here again, the judicial attitude is of utmost value. Even though you favor one side or the other from the beginning, you must make everyone feel that he has had full opportunity to air his views. In such a case, incidentally, it is usually better to state your partisanship in the beginning than to try to pretend impartiality.

You might say, "I am inclined to favor Bill Black's views in this matter, but I want to hear what the rest of you have to say. I think we should hear all angles discussed. It is quite possible that some of us could change our minds." Having done this, give everyone a chance to speak fully. (Of course, you retain the chairman's prerogative of tactfully cutting short the repetitious and too longwinded.)

In chairing any group, you must maintain control. If things get too heated in the informal meeting, you might be wise to insist that anyone who wishes to speak must wait to be recognized. Whatever you do, keep your own temper in rein.

Make Out an Agenda as an Aid to Order

A most useful prop for any chairman of a group is the written agenda. If you have not prepared one ahead of time, do so as soon as you call the meeting to order. In the latter case you may ask the help of those present in deciding on the material to be covered. When the list is finished, keep it before you. It will not only be a reminder of all points to be covered, but you will find it a potent aid to keeping order. A gavel, of course, is also most useful and authoritative. If you have none, rapping sharply with a pencil will often serve the same purpose — but use it sparingly

The Successful Chairman's Attitude

If you are new to the business of being chairman, it does no harm to say so; but do not be facetious. I have seen men make silly spectacles of themselves in such a situation, and lose control of the group immediately. Do not joke. If you feel you must mention your inexperience, just say, "I have been asked to chair the meeting today because Mr. Bingham had another urgent appointment. As you know, I am new at this, so I hope you will all bear with me and give me your fullest cooperation. Will the meeting now come to order? We have an important question to discuss." (Read agenda, or ask for help in preparing one.)

Keep the proceedings rather informal, but maintain dignity. Be careful not to assume a pompous attitude, or you will arouse resentment and probably accomplish very little.

Use These Key Phrases in Meeting-Management

The three main problems in chairing a meeting include keeping order, keeping the members to the subject at hand, and preventing arguments from becoming too heated. Verbal admonitions will usually take care of all three.

In the matter of keeping order and staying on the prescribed subject, phrases like the following are useful. Tap briskly with your pencil to get attention, and say:

- Let's keep to the agenda, ladies and gentlemen (or folks), so that we can finish this meeting in a reasonable time. The point we are discussing is . . . What are your thoughts on this, Jane?

- I think the matters at hand require our full attention. Joe, what do you think about the question of staying open on Sunday?

When heated arguments break out, make sure you control your own temper and keep your voice down. Use the gavel to stop all discussion momentarily, then say something conciliatory, as:

- Let's not get carried away. Let's consider this matter calmly.

- I don't think there is any need for anyone to lose his temper in discussing this subject. Everyone will have a chance to speak. Now, Bob, what was the point you were making? Let everyone hear it, so we can all think about it.

A Cure for Persistent Fractiousness

If the shouting continues or crops up again, it is a good idea to insist that the pros and cons of the question be written down. Use a blackboard if one is available, and delegate the writing job to the noisiest member of the group. Have him make two columns, headed "For" and "Against;" then have him write down the points made as the members of the group are polled.

If you have no blackboard, write down the arguments yourself on a large writing pad that should be part of your equipment. Have Mr. Troublesome read off the points and take a hand vote of the members. If making the decision is up to you alone, you may read off the points and immediately announce your decision — or defer it to another time. When you have made either move, go on resolutely to the next item on the agenda, if there is another item. If everything has been covered, then thank the members at the meeting for their cooperation and thoughtfulness, *no matter how they have behaved,* and immediately adjourn the meeting. You can perhaps suggest that everyone go for coffee, to end on a friendly note.

Remember that *thank you* ranks with *please* as one of the most vital elements in your arsenal of key words and phrases. Both are neglected surprisingly often.

CHAPTER 6

How to Differ Winningly and How to Deal With Enemies

"Young Legislator Upsets N. H. House." You may remember reading that headline about a brash twenty-one-year-old who managed somehow to get elected to the New Hampshire 400-seat House. "I am a confrontation politics person," he is quoted as saying. "If I believe something is right, or I believe something is wrong, I say it and I don't worry about the way I say it, how I say it, or who might be offended or hurt."

Here, in a few simple words, is a perfect recipe for defeat — in business, as well as in politics.

Liberals in the New Hampshire House, who should have been the young legislator's allies, hated to have him on their side. On every hand he reaped enmity, and his powers were shorn.

A prestigious colleague summed up the reasons for it. "He violates the mores, customs, and traditions of the legislature."

Read that again: *He violates the mores, customs, and traditions.* What this means, in simpler language, is that he refused to show good manners and he refused to play according to the rules of the game. He, and a few others like him, in business and elsewhere, appear on the scene briefly and disappear quickly. They just have not done their share of thinking and analysis — perhaps are not equipped to do it.

Play the Game According to the Rules That Win

It should be quite apparent to anyone who turns his mind to such subjects that the "mores, customs, and traditions" of almost any human group have evolved over the years for solid, practical reasons. The fact is that they make the machinery run more smoothly, and they help to control the primitive instincts and emotions which can be disruptive of progress.

The moral of all this is that whether your field is politics or business, the only successful way to play the game, to put yourself across, is to maneuver *within the rules* of the game. For the bold and clever there is ample latitude within these confines. They find it possible to differ without offending — and to differ winningly.

Phrases and Approaches That Make Opponents Receptive

Not in business or anywhere else are you going to persuade anyone to your ideas by the confrontation process — the "head-on" approach. First of all, it is ill-conceived. An argument should be a search for the truth or a search for the best method of doing something, carried on by two or more people who are equally interested in the good of the business.

Do not let any argument become a personal contest between you and the other party. The moment this occurs reasoning is impaired, and all concerned are likely to lose sight of the major objective. More important to you personally, perhaps, is the fact that you are putting yourself in a position in which you may lose face and stature should the decision go against you. If, on the other hand, you win in a personal contest, you will almost surely have engendered bitterness in your opponent.

The next time you need his cooperation, he will be waiting to have at you.

Key Phrases to Use in Differing

In phrasing your reply to a presentation with which you disagree, you should be thoughtful and deliberate. Read over the following introductory phrases and make them your own. Note how each one gives the other speaker full credit for objectivity and intelligence, and yet gracefully introduces your own thoughts.

- You have a good point there, but I have another angle on it that I think we should discuss.
- There is a lot of merit in what you say. We might extend this thinking even further, to the question of . . . Here it does not seem to me that it will work out so well.
- I have a great deal of respect for Mr. Brown's opinion, and I think we should consider it carefully. However, there is another thought that occurs to me . . .
- What you say is interesting, but I think we should discuss this on two planes. You're absolutely right about the savings on the number of employees required, but have you considered what it might cost us in impaired customer-relations? I don't believe we can consider one without the other.

Phrases and Attitudes to Avoid

Remember, in any discussion, that the other fellow just may be right. Give him a full chance to express his ideas and to dissect yours. Do not interrupt or cut him off in the middle of his talk. Not only your opponent, but everyone else present will resent such behavior. In this connection, keep in mind that your object is to persuade, to get your ideas adopted, and to win your opponent's support for them.

After you have made your own exposition and your adversary still disagrees, there is one dangerous phrase which should be avoided like the plague. Never, whatever the situation, say, "You don't understand!"

No phrase could be more of a red flag, except a deliberately rude one. First of all, it is an insult. By saying this the speaker is really saying, in effect, "I am very smart, and I have expressed an idea very clearly, but it is beyond your intelligence to grasp it!"

Boom! The standard reply comes crashing back in a shout. "Of course I understand! I just don't agree!" And when your listener now says he does not agree, nothing will ever budge him from that point of view.

Use This Key Phrase to Promote Understanding

If you truly believe your listener does not understand, then the fault is with you, and you should accept it if you hope to win him over. Instead of insultingly saying, "You don't understand," turn the situation around, and take the opportunity for restatement in clearer fashion. Say, instead, "Well, *I just haven't made myself clear.* What I meant was this . . . " Or, perhaps, say, "I just haven't explained it well. Let me go over it and see if I covered all the advantages, *as I see them.* First of all . . . "

By this simple, gracious device, you have gotten the show on the road again and have given yourself a chance to make a second exposition, with a now sympathetic listener.

I haven't made myself clear. That is a key phrase for anyone dealing with people. Think about it and practice it, so it will come easily when the need for it arises.

Making an Enemy Into a Friend

A book like this that concentrates on solving difficulties sometimes tends to give the impression that all business is a matter of constant contests — that there is no peace. In a very subtle sense this may be true, in that a man who is determined to get ahead, to put himself across, must keep his objective in mind at all times, being careful to present himself in the best light. From an active point of view, it is not true. An encounter with an actual enemy is rather rare.

Perhaps this very rarity makes an encounter with a true, active enemy an unsettling experience, if you are not prepared for it. Handling the situation calls for all the diplomatic skills. Let us consider the various types of enemies.

An Analysis of Enemies You May Encounter

Most numerous, perhaps, is the entrenched assistant to the boss, who is determined to put everyone "in his place." To him, any importance or glory that anyone else achieves is a threat to his own importance.

Similar to him is the man whose duties have been divided, and who now must watch someone else do part of "his job." He fears that your performance may surpass his own in the same field. He does not stop to consider that your performance should be better, since you will have fewer duties.

A third enemy type is the man who is aiming at the same job you have trained your sights upon. Or perhaps he is the lazy incompetent above you, who fears that you may get his job. He usually devotes a good part of his time to politics.

A fourth type is the fellow who just takes a dislike to you on sight — or who automatically treats every newcomer disdainfully until he has "proved" himself.

Last, and perhaps easiest to cope with, is the man you have antagonized through some maladroitness on your part. Here you should apologize, if necessary, and cultivate his good will.

None of the previous four mentioned will ever classify himself as we have done. It is human nature to rationalize and to put oneself in a good light in one's own mind. Each of these men will diligently search for faults in you to justify his enmity, probably doing no self-analysis at all. People like these simply react — and usually with great skill.

How to Handle Some Difficult Opponents

What to do? The first thing to do is to resolve to keep your own composure, and then to undertake a little analysis of your own, so that you can recognize the source of your opponent's attitude.

The first two opponents on the list — the entrenched assistant and the man who had your job — are usually met with when you are new to an organization or department. Luckily they are fairly easy to deal with. Their antagonism is motivated by fear, and your job is to allay that fear, subtly but effectively.

- Treat these antagonists with guileless friendliness at all times, as though you do not even recognize their opposition, so that no open fight can ever develop. (This is a basic technique for dealing with all opposition within the business.)
- Parry any jibes gently, making use of the stalling-for-time phrases, if necessary, while composing your answer. (See Chapter Five.)
- Use deference and skillful flattery to allay their fears. (You can take your cue from the way long-term employees treat them.)
- In reply to a heated question or accusation, use the accuser's first name in a conciliatory reply. "I think, Dick, that such and such . . . " This has a friendly, affectionate effect and also reduces the pomposity of the accuser. Smile gently and speak with patience and dignity.

The flattery referred to can take the form of complimenting a piece of work the person has managed, perhaps complimenting a presentation of some sort, or even something done in the past. Occasionally you can make these flattering comments in an open meeting, and you will see your opponent melt in pleased acceptance. Compliments on clothing and appearance are also sometimes helpful, to a lesser extent.

In the case where you are doing a job that was formerly part of another man's work, and he is afraid you will outdo him, you might make it a point to tell him how well he had everything organized. You might also mention that you don't see how he found time to take care of both projects.

With him, as with the insecure executive assistant, time is your ally. After you have been around for a while and no damage has accrued to him, his attitude will gradually soften.

Combatting an Outright Enemy

The third classification of opponents — the man who is aiming at the same job you are, and the man above you who fears that you are trying for his job — these are more difficult to cope with. You can use on them some of the maneuvers described above, but it is very unlikely that you will ever convert them into friends — especially if you are successful in your ambitions!

The most important thing for you to do in their case is to recognize their antagonism early, so that you can take measures to combat any covert maneuvers against you. If you, discover that there is an out and out campaign against you, then you may want to resort to politics on your behalf. Never, in any case, quarrel with this enemy. Do not show your hand. Work quietly behind the scenes, making friends, selling yourself.

Overloading — Another Enemy Tactic

Unfortunately there is one enemy maneuver that little will avail against, and you may become enmeshed in this trap before you realize it. Being forewarned, you may be able to devise some defense. The enemy device referred to is *overloading,* and many an executive is forced to resign because of it. Even corporation presidents succumb.

The executive above you, or sometimes even the managerial board, carefully plans the victim's demise and keeps the plans secret with elaborate precautions. The victim, who may be a conscientious type and already overworked, finds his duties and responsibilities ever expanding. The more he does, the more work there is added; until at last he makes a spectacular error, or must confess that he cannot cope. Sometimes his enemy or enemies are "sympathetic," but he is either fired or urged to quietly resign.

This diabolical maneuver works best against the new man who has not formed any connections; against the overly ambitious man; and against the man who needs his job desperately. It is a vicious, underhanded thing, and the farther you allow it to go, the less you can do about it. The victim is too busy, too distracted, too overwhelmed with work to realize that he is the victim of a plot, until it is too late. Sometimes he delegates authority, only to find he has chosen an enemy minion who sabotages him.

Ask Questions and Get the Facts

If you ever find yourself in such a situation, the most important thing is to recognize your victimization early. The moment you find that you are being given more to do than any reasonable human being could be expected to do, take time out and act. Go first to the man who is channeling the work to you and cautiously discuss the matter with him, maintaining an attitude of utmost good humor, even naivete, in order to allay any suspicion on his part that you see through the trick. The point of this discussion is to make sure that you actually are being made a victim.

You may find that your tormenter was quite innocent (if a bad administrator) and that he did not realize he was overloading you. In this case he will take steps to remedy the situation, and talk quite reasonably about it. The guilty schemer, on the other hand, will probably reveal his intentions through his critical or uncooperative attitude — never in so many words. In a day or so you may find yourself with even more added work, if you go no further in your protest.

One Occasion to Go to the Top

Your best bet, if you achieve no relief by going to the executive above you, is to then go quietly to the man who hired you, or to the head of the business himself. Introduce your subject by reminding your listener that you know this job thoroughly and are experienced in it, that you came well recommended on your past performance. Then explain to him how your duties have been multiplied beyond all human capability, and ask his assistance in straightening out the matter. You might finish up with a remark something like the following, and await his reaction:

- I can do an excellent job for this company; I have proved that in past performance. However, if I am going to continue to be overloaded in this manner, neither I nor anyone else can guarantee top performance. I don't want my record damaged by this situation, and I do not want the company to suffer. What do you think can be done?

Very quickly now you will know your fate, and you will not go through the ignominy of failing.

Unfortunately, even if you win and your tormenter is brought into line temporarily, you will not be in the best of situations. On the other hand, you may have bought yourself time and some peace of mind, so that you can line up another post in short order.

What to Do About Other Enemy Tactics

Other techniques in the high echelons' bag of underhanded tricks are the Uriah tactic and the "watering down" maneuver.

Both of these, like the overload, can only be successfully defended against if you have many allies in the organization and can launch a strong political maneuver of your own.

The Uriah tactic is to keep you out in the field or busy on trips and assignments so frequently that you no longer know what is going on in the home organization.

In the "watering down" maneuver you may find yourself with a new assistant, or several of them, who take over a large part of your duties and report directly to the man above you. Obviously you are being shorn of power and authority. Unless you are very close to retirement and wish to merely hang on, you may as well begin looking for another job. The exception, of course, is the case in which you yourself have extensive political resources within the organization and can counter-attack.

Avoiding the Ultimatum that Hurts You

In all the situations outlined above, and indeed in any situation in business, it is wise to keep things on a civil, well-mannered basis. There is no point in histrionics or displays of temper. For the most part, if you indulge in these you will almost surely be adding to the enemy's supply of ammunition. Keep your temper and goad him, if you can, into becoming angry and showing his hand openly.

Whatever you do, never lay down an ultimatum. To lay your job on the line or make empty threats is worse than useless. More than ninety-nine times out of one hundred, the job that is laid on the line in an ultimatum is quickly snatched away. Do not present your opponent with this excuse for undue haste. Give yourself time to take care of your own affairs.

As for the matter of vengeance, bide your time. Life has a strange way of bringing things full circle. In the meantime, plan and manage your own future so that you may forget such unhappy incidents, basking in a new success.

Dealing with the Disloyal Employee

A dangerous enemy, but one easily dealt with if you catch up with him in time, is the disloyal employee. The secretary or the assistant who works against you or belittles you in the eyes of others can do a great deal of damage. No matter how skilled or how helpful such an employee is in the matter of work, the best policy is to deal with him summarily. Get rid of him. The best course is to fire him; but do so on some pretext, not revealing the actual reason. Tell him you are forced to cut down on the staff, or even that his work is not satisfactory — any excuse is justified. Such people can be extremely devious, and it has been my observation that they should never be given a second chance. As the Chinese saying goes, "Dog bites man: bad dog. Dog bites man again: bad man."

If your assistant here happens to be the boss' son, you have a greater problem. You may have to try the despicable "overloading" tactic yourself. Then again, you might insist that he be promoted out of your department — preferably to something that will keep him well-occupied.

CHAPTER 7

How to Tell the Boss He Misunderstood—Don't!

You can often get by with only rudimentary knowledge of your job. You can get away with quite a few errors. You can irritate people right and left. You can do all of these things and still hold onto your job sometimes, even though they do not speed your progress. However, there is one thing you cannot do and hope to survive, and that is to fail in getting along with the boss. He is the kingpin, of course. He comes in all sizes, shapes, temperaments, and degrees of intelligence.

I have worked for years for some men with whom I had not the slightest thing in common. Some other men and women have been so compatible that we have been friends for ten, even twenty years since the business connection was severed. Yet with none in either group could I ever truly relax and be myself while I worked with him. I am sure this is true of many, if not most, people who work for a living. The vital necessity of maintaining the equability of the relationship precludes any true sense of ease — yet one dares not give any hint of this watchful nervousness!

Psyching Out a New Superior

The first days with a new boss are probably the most difficult, when both he and the job are strange. You need not worry too much, however, about whether he likes you or not, in the majority of cases, because he is the man who hired you. If he hired you, you at least are not a type that repels him. Now to keep it that way!

The best plan, I have observed, is to go easy during the first few days or weeks, until you really know your man. Be pleasant, be cheerful, but keep wit and clever sallies to a minimum. Sense of humor varies greatly from one individual to another; some people actually feel threatened if you make a joke that they do not understand. Others may decide that you are not serious enough about the tremendous importance of the gigantic project they head up — whether it is manufacturing shoelaces or building suspension bridges.

Go slow. Even if the boss himself is a jokester, don't reply in kind or, least of all, try to top him. Just laugh appreciatively where it is required. Men reach the top by various routes, and some are not overly burdened with either brains or wit. Some I have known, and you probably have, too, are certain that because they are in a high place they have proven their superiority in every phase of human talent. This includes both wit and the highly specialized work it took you years to learn.

Note How Others Treat Him

Be wary. Psych out your man. Listen to him. Study him, and listen to the way long-term employees treat him. By and large, their way with the man probably represents the type of behavior he likes best, or even demands. Do not be misled by fiction to the contrary.

An incident in the TV series, *"The Odd Couple,"* illustrates my point. In this episode, Oscar "stood up" to a loud, domineering boss who had just fired Felix. "Just a minute, you can't fire him," he said — or words to that effect. "He's a wonderful artist and a valuable man. Whatever happened was my fault."

"Good!" exclaimed the domineering one. "I like a man who stands up for his friends! YOU'RE FIRED, TOO!"

That is about the way it goes in real life. If only toadies surround a particular executive, it is not because they all prefer to spend their lives in genuflection. You will have to either join them, if you hope to work for him, or look for the nearest exit.

Luckily for those of us born with backbone, such executives, amounting to caricatures, are few and far between. Yet you will be wise to give all those above you the respect to which their position entitles them, or to which they feel entitled. Above all, keep your arsenal of key words and phrases handy. Remember at all times that your most important job is to sell yourself.

Make a Friend of the Boss

The sooner you can make a friend of the man you work for, the better. Note his interests and study up on them, so that you can comment intelligently and understand his stories. If you intend to stay with the company for a long time, it might even pay you to take up golf or to brush up on your bridge techniques with a few lessons. Keep your eyes and your ears open for opportunities to show interest. Bring in a news clipping or a cartoon occasionally to illustrate a point he has made.

Offer to do a favor now and then, if you think it will be appreciated. Better still, ask a favor! Strangely enough, the very idea that he can do you a favor, or that you want him to, warms the heart of the average human being. A simple thing like lending you a book he has liked, or bringing in a small art object you have wanted to see — of such things are friendships made. The man who does the favor gets a special feeling of importance, and a flush of pleasure that comes from sharing an interest or in being appreciated.

It goes without saying, of course, that you should never presume on this friendship. Be careful to show respect at the proper times, and do not allow your friendliness to become an embarrassment. Be careful not to let yourself appear to be teacher's pet.

Pointers on Working for a Woman

A special word of warning should go to the man who finds himself in the rare situation of working for a woman. Do not be misled by the James Bond tales and other such wishful male fiction. Every woman is *not* dying to have you make love to her. About the quickest way in the world to have a woman executive fire you is for you to insist on making passes at her, or to persist in amorous or suggestive behavior.

This is not to say that you should not pay a compliment now and then, or let the woman boss know that you admire her as a woman; but keep it cool, and keep hands off. The competent female executive is insulted, even infuriated, by the mere hint that a physical attraction to you might influence her judgment of your work. Moreover, she must guard her reputation as a woman and as an executive.

Compliment the Woman Boss Cautiously

Here are some samples of permissible compliments, to be used rather sparingly:

- Oh! A new hairdo. Looks great!
- My! You're looking lovely and cool on this hot day!
- I like your new outfit. Very becoming.
- Pink is one of your best colors. You look great.

Avoiding Misunderstandings

Because neither of you knows the other, communication is sometimes a real problem during the first weeks with a new superior. When you have something to say, say it slowly and clearly, in full detail. Be on the alert for possible problems in semantics. Terms that mean one thing to you may mean something else in the new organization.

The semantics problem can be particularly acute in the electronics industry, for instance, where the same job can go by many different names. When you are talking to the new boss, make sure you are both basing your comments on the same thing. Make yourself clear.

An example of what I mean is rather far afield, but shows what difficulties language can cause. A young woman cousin of mine once found herself with an English boyfriend. She thought he was charming, until he told her he liked her so much because she was so *homely*! It took him quite a while to find out that he should have said, in America, that it was because she was home-loving or homey.

In dealing with the boss, new or old, everything that has been said about tact goes double. If you often have trouble getting along with superiors, go back and read Chapters Five and Six again. You may want to review them a number of times until the techniques and phrases that are given become second nature.

How to Correct the Boss Acceptably

There are occasions, of course, in any organization, when your superior will be in error, or on the verge of making a serious mistake. He will appreciate it if you save him from his folly — but only if you do it in a way that allows him to save face. Commit these useful lead-in phrases to memory now, so that they will come to mind quickly when you need them:

- Just a minute, Mr. Jones, if I may interrupt. *I think I may have misled you there.* I neglected to point out some of the adverse effects in this area. Take the matter of . . .

  Or (in another case) the Smith Company tells us that deliveries cannot be made on time for our purposes.

  (Note that you do *not* tell him he misunderstood. See Chapter Six.)

- I am certainly intrigued by your plan, Mr. Jones, but there are a couple of little points I wish we could discuss. For instance . . .

- I'm sure this is not new to you, but I think it might have some application to the plan. The question is, "How can we cope with it?" I'm speaking of the difficulty of re-tooling each season (or whatever).

In the last two approaches you are pretending to accept the plan, but actually you are shoving it back into the category of unfinished business and opening it up for discussion. You compliment the man, yet try to get him to think about obstacles or weaknesses. What you treat as little points may be major obstacles. It is not necessary to describe them as such. The only need is to create the opportunity to discuss them.

Avoid a Superior Attitude

The attitude to avoid is any indication that you think you know more about the situation than the boss does (even if it is true). If you take this approach you are likely to be squelched, because you have created a personal contest. Make your comments more the tentative musings of a thoughtful listener — which another thoughtful man will want to consider. Once you have dissected the subject, other more timid types will probably support your objections. In any case, you have done your duty and you have not endangered your personal relationship with the man above you.

If, in spite of your gentle approach, your objections are brushed aside by an autocratic or impulsive executive, you may want to make a further effort in the cause of reason. You might want to be more definite, demanding action because of dangers you can see. Again, be careful to avoid the personal contest. Here are a couple of phrases that will probably achieve your purpose:

- Could we throw this on the table a moment for discussion? There are a couple of angles that are just not clear to me

  The answer here may be, "What? What are you talking about? What's not clear?"

Your reply should be slow and deliberate: "Well, I think in the main that the plan sounds great; but I am just wondering about the matter of logistics. Can we assemble material in time to make your deadline? Part 87 comes from Japan, for instance."

Back-Tracking or Reversing Gears to Get on the Right Side

Some executives, who often talk a great deal about the importance of working as a team, are truly autocrats, and demand complete approval of any proposal they make. If you want to stick around, you may as well agree. Sometimes you can do it with reservations, and thus have a slight chance of opening up discussion. Here is one approach:

- I think it sounds great. I can see some possible problems, but nothing that we can't handle.

If this mildly expressed doubt brings down wrath on your head, you may as well subside into silence. There are people who can back-track in such a situation, or even do a complete flip-flop. These are some techniques I have seen them use to divert the dictator's wrath:

- "What? What? I didn't mean that! I guess I didn't make myself clear. I'm 100 percent for the plan!"
- "Wait a minute! I guess I didn't understand the question. Will you repeat it?" And then, when the question is repeated: "Oh, of course I agree! I just didn't understand the question."

Fortunately for employees' self-respect, few top men require such submission.

Parrying the Unexpected Question — Useful Phrases

Some executives have a distressing habit of suddenly pouncing on you with an important question when your mind is a thousand miles away. You may have been immersed for days in figuring costs on a new campaign, when the boss suddenly claps you on the shoulder and demands, "Why did you tell Johnson & Company we could give them number 870 in black and green in time for their convention?"

Your mind goes blank, and you are sure for a minute that you have committed a fatal error. You may feel like an idiot, without a word to say. The solution here is not to panic. Just state the facts as they are, and give yourself time.

- It will take me a moment to answer that — I am so immersed in these figures. Let me get my file.
- I haven't thought about that for so long, you will have to give me a minute. I will look up the records.

  If your inquisitor says that he has Johnson on the phone and wants to give him the information immediately, suggest that *you* call Johnson back in a few minutes. Say, "I want to be sure of the facts, and I have to refresh my memory." Do not be rushed into embarrassment or possible error.

Questions out of the blue are not the only ones that can shake you up, if you allow them to. Sometimes a pat answer is demanded on a really involved or important question. Here the "stalling for time" phrases can be used to give you time to assemble your thoughts, or to think of a graceful way to defer answering. The following are often helpful:

- Well, it's a combination of many things, rather difficult to summarize. Take the matter of . . .
- What does it mean to say . . . ?
- The difficult part is how to define it. Let me think a moment.
- Let me think a moment. It's been a long time, and I want to be accurate.
- Let me think about it a minute. I am not sure that I can answer completely without looking at my records.

Handling the Snooper Boss

One of the most irritating people to work for is the snooper boss, who wants to know what you are doing every minute. He is usually found in small outfits, but his counterpart is often a department head in a larger organization. He follows you on your coffee break, he pokes among your papers when you leave the office, he may even follow you to the washroom.

If he gets on your nerves, try sweetly talking things over with him on every occasion when he does his snooping. It may or may not cure him, but at least it will give you an idea of his motivations. If he thinks you are wasting time, you can either change your ways or perhaps change his opinion.

Try Questioning Him Tactfully

One of the nicest men I ever worked for was a snooper. If he did not follow me out of the office, I found him rummaging around my desk when I returned. After a couple of years of this, and never being able to get any information from him concerning it, I finally decided he was just lonely! I cite this merely to indicate that finding your boss is a snooper does not necessarily indicate that you are suspect, or being subtly criticized for too much time out. The only way to find out his motives is to question him. The following approaches can be helpful:

- (At the desk) Watch the search quietly for a few seconds, then say, "Is there anything I can help you find?"

- (If he follows you on the coffee break) "Do you need me for something? You can always page me if you do, you know." If he says no, you are not needed, then ask if you can get him a cup of coffee. You might add, "Sit down. I have been wanting to talk to you about that Anderson situation, and maybe this is a good time."

The one thing not to do is to put up with the snooping for any period of time, until you become really angry about it. Find out from HIM, not others, what he has on his mind.

Avoid Questioning Associates
About the Boss

If you question others about such a situation, you can only harm yourself and find out nothing. As soon as you leave the person you have questioned, a chain of gossip will probably start, and no good can come of it. He will turn to the next man and say, "Hey! Perkins says Mr. Big follows him on his coffee break and searches through his papers every time he gets a chance. What do you make of it?"

In nine cases out of ten the answer will probably be malicious, human nature being what it is. Perhaps, "Why not? He probably wonders what that guy does all day, besides drinking coffee. I'd like to know, myself." You have heard this sort of thing, so do not make yourself the brunt of it. Ask Mr. Big himself.

The Baiting Boss

Some executives, for no good reason, take pleasure in baiting and trying to embarrass certain people on the staff. It usually means nothing. It may even be their idea of humor.

If you are a victim of this, do not let it upset you. Reply pleasantly and reasonably — perhaps with a touch of simple wit, when apropos.

An important commercial artist I knew was often the butt of the advertising manager's harassment. Like many commercial artists, she kept files of clippings to help with certain problems, and to suggest various techniques that might be used. These files of clippings lying around her office were a constant annoyance to the manager. He never thought to ask about their purpose — just complained about them whenever he saw them. "Why do you have this trash around?" "Why don't you get rid of this messy junk?" "What are you doing? Building a nest?"

Betty, the artist, was an imperturbable type. She just told him, over and over again, that she needed the material, and then changed the subject. One day, however, she really shut him up with the old technique of answering a question with a question. This day the baiter's question was, "Why don't you get rid of this stuff? What would you do with it in case of fire?"

Betty turned her big blue eyes on him and asked solemnly, "Oh, Mr. Big! Are you expecting another fi-uh?"

Mr. Big, who had been involved (as a spectator and bucket-brigader) in one fire, was horrified at the implications of her question. "No, of course not!" he snapped as he stomped out, amid laughter from the grandstand.

Of course this sort of ego-bruising put-down is not recommended, unless you happen to be an invaluable blue-eyed female artist.

The Impossible Boss and the Day that Never Comes

No matter how badly you want to keep your job, no matter how skillfully you employ the techniques of getting along with people, you may, unfortunately, run into the impossible boss. The occasion is rare and unlikely, but it can happen. Nothing pleases him. Nothing you say is understood. From the day you start you are headed for disaster, and you can feel it in your bones. What to do, as a last ditch effort, to save your post?

Examine Yourself for Causes

I would say that the first thing to do at this point is to commune with yourself in private. Examine your methods and make sure that it is not some antipathy of your own or some ineptness that has created the impasse. If, after thorough examination, you decide that you have indeed tied up with the impossible boss, then you will be justified and wise in trying just about any technique. If all is going to be lost anyway, then emergency measures and experimentation are in order.

One way is to ask for a private conference with the man, and to throw the problem on the table between you. Start out by reminding him of your qualifications for the job, perhaps quoting from the letter that got you the job. After a brief introduction of this sort, tell him how disturbed you are that the two of you do not seem to be able to hit it off. Ask him what he thinks the problem is, and frankly tell him your side of it. You may, just may, be able to arrive at an understanding. If not, nothing is lost, because you had nothing to lose.

The day that never comes? That is the day when you tell the impossible boss exactly what you think of him!

How often have you heard a friend say, or said it yourself, "Some day I am going to tell that fool . . . that scoundrel . . . that s.o.b. exactly what I think of him!" Best advice here is, DON'T DO IT, because it is pointless. It can hurt you later, perhaps haunt you for years, when future employers call to make inquiries about you.

Do it when you are retiring on your first million? Or when you have won the Irish Sweepstakes? No. Not even then. What is the point in marring a happy farewell party?

CHAPTER 8

Learn to Say, "I Goofed" —
There is Power
in Some Humility

Some philologists claim that the slang we all use occasionally tends to impoverish the language and stunt the vocabulary. This may be true. From my viewpoint, however, slang has virtues far removed from aesthetic literature, and a valuable function all its own. Certain slang terms here and there have no real substitute in the language, and they have done immeasurable service in easing human relationships, in cutting events and people down to size.

I witnessed a dramatic example of this while I was working as retail ad manager for the same "impossible" boss mentioned in the previous chapter.

Few business processes are more pressured, more tense, more easily thrown into a frenzy than retail advertising, with its relentless day-to-day deadlines. Observing the well-organized, often clever retail advertising that is produced, it would be hard to imagine the complications that enter into its production — the reams of data that must be processed, infused with creativity, translated into type and illustrations, checked and re-checked every single day. Add to this the veloxes and engravings and type that must be ordered; the scores of human beings who must be dealt with.

Considering it all, surprisingly few errors are committed — yet when an error does slip by, all hell breaks loose. Money is involved! Store prestige and reputation are involved. Finding an immediate solution is involved — because the catastrophe pertains to today, right now!

Buyers, merchandise managers, and top brass descend on the advertising department in wild excitement. Shouting and accusations rend the air, and much time is wasted trying to decide whose fault the error was. The only good thing about the commotion is that it reaches a crescendo in a half hour or so, and then subsides when a solution is arrived at or some process decided upon.

An Example of Slang's Usefulness

In the particular job I speak of, the store owner was a man who just loved an excuse for an explosion and for setting everybody on his ear. On one particular occasion (a rare one) when a wrong price crept through and got into the paper, the big boss was in fine form and tore the place apart. I missed it, luckily or unluckily, because of a dental appointment; but when I came in about ten my frazzled assistant gave me a blow-by-blow description.

Since the problem had already been disposed of and quiet reigned, I told her to forget it; and we settled down to the next daily outpouring.

Mr. Vesuvius still hoped for a little more excitement, however, and he dashed in and pounced on me as soon as he heard I was in. "Did you hear about the error in the men's wear ad?" he challenged, eyes glinting.

"Yes," I sighed. "Marie told me about the flap."

The slang expression was new, and it hit him between the eyes.

"The *flap?*" he queried. And then he laughed. "It was a flap all right! It was a flip-flap!"

All the steam was gone. The colorful slang word had caught his fancy, with its apt connotation of chickens flapping wildly, squawking, and running in all directions. He chuckled over it as he went out.

I chalked up one for slang.

The Greatest of All Slang Phrases — A Key Phrase

"No sweat" is another wonderful slang phrase that has saved many a day. There will be others, too, created by that clever fellow Anonymous and presented to us to save strain and contribute perspective. The greatest slang creation of all times, however, is the marvellous *"I goofed."*

Before the advent of this magic phrase, strong men and virtuous women by the millions found it absolutely impossible to admit error. Countless hours were spent in circumlocution, in fruitless charges and countercharges and heated arguments. When at last the culprit was pinned down, and had to utter the hated words, "I made a mistake," he sweated and writhed, and cringed as though he were throwing himself on a rack of nails.

Suddenly all that changed. What was so difficult became easy with this slightly humorous phrase; and strangely enough, a goof-up is much more quickly forgiven and forgotten than an old-fashioned mistake.

"I goofed" indicts humanity as well as one's self. It says, in effect, "I am human, and all of us humans goof occasionally. You have goofed, he has goofed some time or another; now I have done it."

The automatic answer seems to be, "Okay, just so you don't do it again, or do it too often;" and everyone concerned can get down to the business of correcting the error or making any adjustments called for.

If you are one of those who still find it difficult to admit that you made a mistake, learn to say, "I goofed." It rolls easily off the tongue. Its pronouncing causes scarcely a ripple. And you will be better-liked for having joined the error-prone human race.

Nobody Loves Mr. Right — Don't Dodge Responsibility

Nobody loves Mr. Right, the guy who is never wrong — chiefly because he is a phony. He thinks of himself as strong, yet actually he is weak; and perhaps he knows this, deep inside himself. Bluster and bad temper dare anyone to accuse him of error. When he does err he tries desperately to cover up, or to blame his mistake on someone else. He feels that his image and even his true self will be destroyed if he is found out.

In one sense he is indeed right.

If you try to cover up a misstep or blame it on someone else, you magnify its importance. Sometimes you will get away with it, but eventually some error will catch up with you. If you have made a big thing of it by dodging and denial, the revelation that you are in truth the culprit may prove devastating.

Don't Dramatize an Error

The big point here is that an error in any business causes enough dislocation just by its existence. Do not magnify it by trying to dodge responsibility or shift the blame. The thing to do is to face it, admit it, and dispose of it as quickly as possible.

This does not mean that you should minimize the error, if it is a serious one. On the contrary, you should state the seriousness of the matter at the same time as you make your admission. It is much better for you to do so than to wait for someone else to state it. If you have not completely wrecked the organization, your honesty and contrition tend to allay some of the wrath against you. If, at the same time, you can suggest a solution or the possibility of a solution, you may save a great deal of commotion and over-emphasis.

Use Approaches Like These in Admitting Errors

The following phrases fit varying situations. Study them and think about them now, so that they can serve you in case of need:

- You are right. I seem to have goofed. Let's see what we can do to straighten things out.

- I hate to tell you, Mr. Big, but I seem to have goofed on my estimate. I called Green & Company to stop work on the project (if a wise action), until you could decide what you think we should do.

- In re-checking my figures, Mr. Big, I find that I made a slight error. The difference is about $80.00. We could make it up in some degree by changing the grade of paper — to, say a 50 percent rag instead of an 80 percent. Here are some samples of the two grades. What do you think?

In the last suggestion you have presented a possible solution at the same time you admitted your error, so that you have given Mr. Big something to think about besides the mistake. You may escape with only a perturbed comment on the part of Mr. Big. On the other hand, he may still pounce on you in fury. If he does, your best bet is to agree with his censure, and try to get back to the solution.

You may wish to present your excuse, if there is one, but do not do it in a combative manner. You want to soothe the situation, not aggravate it. Use the power of humility. The good old Biblical admonition, *Agree with thine adversary quickly,* applies here.

Some suggested replies:

- Yes, it was a stupid goof-up. I'm not excusing myself, but I did have to figure it in the midst of that terrific rush last week. What do you think we can do about it now?

- I don't blame you for being angry. I am going to put a double check on these things hereafter. I think I can sell Smith & Sons on the change in the paper, if they don't want to pay the difference.

Correcting Your Own Error

The fact that you should admit an error frankly and quickly when you have to does not mean that you should go out of your way to sacrifice yourself. There are occasions when you can catch your own error and correct it, without causing a general dislocation.

Long ago, when I was doing a sort of one-man job of promotion for a church organization, I found myself in this situation. In this job I not only had to write the ads, but after they were printed I had to address the envelopes and send them out! I had just dispatched about three hundred sales letters to Army, Navy, and prison chaplains, when I discovered to my horror that I had forgotten to enclose the separate sheet that included the order blank and the price list. What to do?

Since the waste created (if any) was only my time, the cost of extra envelopes, and about fifteen dollars in postage, I saw no point in mentioning the error. I merely set about addressing and stuffing another three hundred envelopes — punishment enough for me, considering my loathing of clerical work. When they were finished, I shipped the job out.

Not only did I receive no censure from the low-budget organization, but sales were sensational! The hymnals I was trying to sell in my letter had gathered dust on the shelves for years, and no one had been able to move them. In this case we sold every last one — thousands of them! I am sure the extra few dollars spent on making the double impression on our prospects was an important factor. Whether the extra items of expense were ever discovered no one ever told me.

Defending Against the Harpy

In some organizations there are sacred cow characters who specialize in loudly calling attention to other people's errors. I say it reluctantly, but more women than men fall into this category. The instant these self-appointed sentinels are apprised of someone's mistake, they attack like screaming harpies out of the blue, shouting accusations for all to hear. Sometimes they have taken their news to the top man first, and bring him along to witness your hoped-for annihilation.

It is not that the harpy hates you particularly. She may; but usually her only purpose is to appear important, and to show how capable and accurate she is by highlighting your stupidity and carelessness. Defending against her calls for an entirely different technique from those described above. Your object should be twofold: one, to bring your error into perspective; two, to deflate the harpy.

The most satisfying denouement is to be able to show that the harpy is mistaken — that there was no error. Next best is to point out that the error has already been found and attended to. If you are not in either lucky position, proceed carefully.

Refuse to Get Excited — Use These Key Phrases

First of all, do not let the harpy rattle you or get *you* excited. You might even refuse to listen until she lowers her voice and states the situation calmly. Phrases like the following are usually effective. Remember them, because they will help you to keep your temper.

- I can't hear you when you shout like that. Can you tell me calmly what you are talking about?
- Sit down and calm down. You are likely to have a stroke if you excite yourself like this. Now! What's the problem?
- Please, Miss H., lower your voice. I can't understand

a word that you are saying. Please show me now just what it is that has gotten you into such a flap.

Such phrases put your attacker on the defensive for an instant, giving you time to consider the error she has found and what to do about it. As in other circumstances, face up to the facts calmly and proceed with the solution. Do not shout; do not dramatize. Just treat the mistake as something that happens willy-nilly now and then, and attend to it. Since it is in your field of competence, you can often show that the correction is a simple matter. Approaches similar to the following are usually effective. Study them.

- Yes, somebody seems to have goofed here. I'm sorry. Let's see what we can do about it.
- Yes. You are right. I have goofed. But I think I can take care of it without causing any real damage. Will you excuse me? I will call John, and then I will call you and let you know how we work it out.
- Yes, I see I omitted one zero here, but I don't think any great harm has been done. I am sure the order has not been shipped. I'll shoot off a wire to Smith & Company as soon as you leave.
- Yes. I goofed. I'll have to take care of this right away. It reminds me of the time you goofed up the Fitzgerald matter and almost lost that account for us. Thanks for letting me know in time.

The harpy is never cured, because she has problems. However, if you deprive her of her drama, she may think twice next time before she chooses you as her victim.

Pointing Out Another's Error to Him

With the terrible example of the harpy in mind, stop and think a moment before you rush to point out another man's error. Remember that it is just as important to keep the peace and preserve friendly feelings as it is to set things right.

If the man is available when the error comes to light, go directly to him, not over his head, and choose your words. Try *not* to put him on the defensive or make him angry. The following phrases are examples of good approaches to this ticklish problem. Study them.

- I'm not sure you had all the facts, Bill, when you drew up this report; but I see something I think may be wrong. Do you want to go over it with me?
- I hope you didn't, John, but I think you might have goofed on these figures for Brown & Company. I get a different total. Do you want to check me?
- I was about to give Mr. Big this estimate of yours for Jones Brothers, when I noticed you have included part no. 482. Wasn't that discontinued last month? Have you got the new parts sheet?
- Joe, I was looking over this catalog sheet of yours, and I think you had better check it before it goes out. The garments you describe don't sound like the ones J. B. was telling me about. Why don't you call and see if they are in the stockroom now, so we can be sure? It's easy to get these models confused.
- Bob, do you want to look up your file copy on that Smith & Company order? Henry Smith just called me, and he says there has been some mistake. He said they didn't order half the stuff they got. Will you check it out and let me know what's up? I told him I would call him back in about fifteen minutes, and I want to know what I am talking about.

Give the Other Fellow an Out to Keep His Good Will

In all these cases you have approached the man as a friend, and carefully avoided an accusing tone. You have given him a chance to find his own error, and in some cases you have suggested an excuse.

Giving the other fellow an out is important. It keeps him

from feeling trapped and compelled to fight. By managing the situation well, you show true executive caliber. And who knows? You may start a trend toward the sensible handling of errors throughout the organization!

CHAPTER 9

The Importance of Culture— How to Polish Your Image Quickly

There is a strange thing about this world of ours. By and large all people are alike, reacting similarly to the same stimuli, pursuing almost identical family lives, and yet they live on different levels. In some areas there is no communication whatsoever between varying groups. You may not realize this, may not even think about it, unless you are suddenly yanked out of one subculture and plunged into another.

A man catapulted upward in a business on the basis of his sales figures or his organizing ability may suddenly find himself seated among utter strangers. In the first upper echelon meeting he attends, small talk and joshing eddy around him, but he sits tongue-tied. The language he hears sounds like English, but it might as well be Hindi or Tagalog as far as he is concerned. The new group's favorite sports and chief interests are completely foreign to him. Ordinarily poised and as sociable as the next fellow, he shrinks now and begins to fear that someone will ask him a question.

Some Temporary Dodges that Can Save You

If there has just been a heavyweight championship fight or a sensational no-hitter in baseball, a self-possessed man may get by once or twice by shifting the conversation to these; but he cannot use this dodge forever. Let's face it. If you wish to stay a part of the in-group, you must share their interests, be able to speak their language.

There is scarcely a meeting of big men anywhere that does not start out with talk on subjects far afield. Hobbies and outside interests are like a secondary theme that runs all through the background of business association.

How I Solved My Own Predicament

I had a rather startling experience of being shifted from one business subculture to another when I was a youngster, and I have always been thankful that it happened to me at an early age. I came from an educated family, but outside of personal doings among the many members, our table talk was usually of politics, ethics, and the law. (My father was a lawyer.) In business, on the other hand, I had up to this time been associated with clerks, stenographers, and such. Suddenly I was given an opportunity in advertising, and was shifted out of this community.

From the work angle everything was fine; however, in personal contacts with the new group I began to feel like an ignorant bumpkin. My co-workers' talk very often was of music, opera, and ballet. They assumed that everyone was acquainted in these fields; and I had nothing to say. They had hit my blind spot.

Oddly enough, my mother was musical, but I had been born tone-deaf! Music, to me, was just loud noise — often a dreadful cacophony to my over-sensitive ears. Consciously or unconsciously I had shut out all experience in this area. Now

I could either try to make up for lost time or remain a boob, with no one to talk to. I decided on the first course, being dogged and proud by nature.

First off, I brought a season ticket to the famous Philadelphia Orchestra, under the great Leopold Stokowski. Thenceforth, week after week, every Saturday, I sat in the gallery in agony, while the storms of glorious music broke over me, meaningless and LOUD! Wagner, Beethoven, Ravel, Rimsky-Korsakov . . . they all sounded alike to me. Just noise, like someone hitting a boiler, more or less.

Gradually, however, the miracle took place, thanks to the Maestro's genius, and to some of his concerts for children, which I also attended. I began to hear music as music! I began to recognize the themes, pick out the various instruments; and then, finally, to differentiate among the composers. Attending the orchestra performances became a pleasure rather than a duty, and I went on to enjoy opera and ballet. As a bonus, I could even TALK about them — or, at least, listen intelligently. (Unfortunately, I still cannot carry a tune!)

Proof that Anyone Can Adapt

I cite this rather amazing bit of personal history just to point up the fact that it is true what Archie Moore says — "ANY BOY CAN!" If I could learn to hear music, then anyone can learn anything. So get busy.

The hardest job of accommodation, I imagine, befalls the man brought up in a pragmatic, non-intellectual family, who has been "tone-deaf" to all cultured pursuits. Yet even he can catch up rather quickly, to a point where he is not completely ignorant on topics discussed. It is just a matter of breaking into a new field of self-education. The library will be a great help; but the important thing is to get started immediately.

Some Pointers on Catching Up Quickly

As an example, if the talk is of art and painters, first supply yourself with a book that more or less covers the field — perhaps a history of art in the western world (there are a number of one-volume texts on the subject). Follow up with a book on modern painters, and another on the old masters. Afterward, you may wish to proceed to books on certain individual painters. In all cases, of course, you should choose volumes that are illustrated with quantities of large color plates, so that you can become familiar with the paintings themselves.

In addition to the above books, Lord Kenneth Clark's *"Civilisation"* should help to give you background and a panoramic view. Somewhere along the way you might even want to peruse a book or two on painting techniques.

For panoramic views in other fields, dip into the marvellous series of works by Will and Ariel Durant. You will be amazed at how quickly you can pick yourself out of the category of ignoramus, and feel quite at home listening to discussions in areas that were once completely strange to you.

In the field of music, modern stereo and the wealth of great classical records available in any good music store make it easy to educate the ear and the taste. Learning to appreciate the works that have endured, of course, does not mean that you must forsake your former loves. If you have been a country music buff, by all means stay with it. Simply add another facet to your knowledge.

What to Say If You Are Ignorant in One Area

In the meantime, before you have had a chance to catch up, do not allow yourself to feel inferior. Remember, everyone cannot know everything. If you are confronted with a direct question on a topic of which you are ignorant, do not try to bluff. It never works. There are a number of useful phrases that deal with the situation gracefully. Learn them now and have them ready. Try one of the following that seems suitable to the occasion:

- No. That's one field in which I am completely ignorant. I have been doing a little reading on it, though, and I hope to catch up. (The simple truth. The use of it denotes poise.)

- I just realized how ignorant I am in the field of classical music. I'm going out tonight and invest in some records. Now, if you had asked me about rock or jazz, I could give you an opinion!

- I guess I am just a practical guy who has been out in the field too long. I am going to have to catch up.

- I am not at all knowledgeable in this area, but I am learning. What is your opinion? (Or) If you could recommend some books to me, I would appreciate it.

Whatever you do, never deride the other man's interest or knowledge. Such an attitude will not only irritate him, but will be recognized instantly as the ignorant bravado that it is. It will stamp you at once as a boor and a clod.

Learn Their Games, Speak Their Language

In some executive groups an interest in sports that are new to you may shut you out, if you are unfamiliar with them. It is obviously quite a bit easier to become familiar with these than with the whole cultural picture. Just make haste to expand your sports interests to include them.

Rich men's sports like yachting or polo may be beyond your reach, but even in these areas you can read up on the history of the sports and become knowledgeable about techniques. If some friendly enemy happens to remark upon your sudden expertise, do not be perturbed. Here again, the truth can only do you good.

Good-natured, even chuckling replies like the following show poise, and mark you as a man who is alert and interested in what is going on around him:

- Well, all this talk of sailing got me intrigued. I never realized there was so much to the art of sailing until I started looking into it. Makes me feel like buying a boat.

- Well, I like to know what's going on! Now that I have started looking into it, I can understand your interest.

- Listen! I am finding it so interesting I wish I had looked into it before. My dad used to be quite an expert.

The same poised approach applies to new areas in your work, incidentally. Since different companies line up duties differently under the same title, you may find that your knowledge is lacking in some areas. Face the situation in the same frank manner, but set about remedying the lack immediately. Remarks on this order can help you out of an awkward spot:

- Procedure at Brown & Company was a little different, but I feel that your method is better. I am brushing up on it.
- I am not too familiar with this area, but I am planning to get over to the factory on Wednesday. I'll spend the day there and really get the feel of the system.
- Yes, I am finding that I have to adapt a bit here and there. I have been studying your manuals, however, and I find it will not be much of a problem.

In these you may recognize a technique we have discussed before. You admit a deficiency casually, so as not to give it too much emphasis or importance; but at the same time you present a solution. Even if you have to say, "I realize this is important," you can follow it up with the solution and thus cut the thing down to size.

The Importance of Good English and Good Manners

These possible problems we have just discussed may be encountered by almost anyone who is suddenly promoted into a rarefied environment. In addition to these, there are other problems that may make top-rank success almost impossible to achieve for the self-made man or the uneducated man, unless he quickly does something about them. One of these is the matter of speaking good English. The other pertains to basic good manners and the practice of all the little refinements of courtesy that might have been lacking in his background.

The time to start remedying these deficiencies is, of course, at the very beginning of your career. A surprising number of men, however, arrive in the top ranks and either fall back or never quite make it because of these minus factors. Their work may be excellent, but they are just not the type of men who can be introduced into top social circles. Indeed, their deficiencies in grammar and easy good manners may make it difficult for them to even impress their associates with their ideas.

How You Can Remedy Failings Quickly

Do not think for one moment that these lacks cannot be overcome. They can, and fairly quickly if you apply yourself. The main thing is to recognize your handicap and do something about it.

I once met a young woman who was making her way upward rapidly in the business world, and her reply to a question of mine absolutely astonished me. Miriam, we will call her, spoke beautifully modulated, flawless English. The quality of her voice and her cultured tones were a delight to the listener. As she spoke to me at some length, I kept trying to place her diction geographically — to decide where she had come from. I finally decided upon Boston, although I was not 100 percent sure, because she lacked the too-flat a's and the added r's of Boston. Finally I had to ask her.

"Miriam," I said, "your diction is so beautiful. Where did you come from? Boston?"

"No!" she laughed. "I am German, and when I arrived in the United States six months ago, I spoke only a few words of English."

The explanation for the flawless diction, she explained matter-of-factly, was schooling. As soon as she arrived in New York she had enrolled in an intensive English course and applied herself. Listening to the beautiful off-hand ease with which she spoke our language, it was hard to believe, and yet it was true. Others who knew her vouched for it.

How sad it is, I have thought in later years, that some Americans themselves do not take advantage of such tutoring. There are language schools and speech clinics in almost every great city, and some of the universities offer suitable courses. If you feel uncertain in the use of the language, either spoken or written, you will be doing yourself an inestimable favor by signing up for an intensive course. If a foreigner can achieve what Miriam, a German girl did, certainly a native-born American can do as well.

How You Can Tell You Need Help

How can you tell whether your English is bad, whether your diction needs improving? Talking is almost as natural as breathing, and most people are so used to the speech of their families and the friends they grew up with that they take it for granted that the speech they have heard most frequently is correct. To get away from this pitfall, you must learn to listen to the manner of speech as well as to what is being said.

If your new associates among executives sound markedly different as a group, if their sentence structure is different and they use words that do not come easily to your tongue, chances are you need some brush-up work on your own speech.

An Easy Test

The following little test should help you decide whether or not your English is a handicap to you. Do the test before you look at the answers. On a separate sheet of paper write down the numbers from 1 to 12, leaving space opposite each for a letter or a *yes* or *no*. Now answer the questions quickly and honestly. Write your answers on your answer sheet, so you can throw it away if your score is too bad!

1. Do your new companions in the main seem like snobs? (Answer yes or no.)

2. Is their conversation rather affected? (Answer yes or no.)

3. Do they use quite a few words you rarely if ever use? (Yes or no.)

4. Is their pronounciation of many words different from yours? (Yes or no.)

5. Which do you say?
   a. He doesn't know.
   b. He don't know.

6. Which do you say?
   a. He done it wrong.
   b. He did it wrong.

7. Which do you say?
   a. Leave go of it.
   b. Let go of it.

8. Which do you say?
   a. He just lay there.
   b. He just laid there.

9. Which do you say?
   a. Like he was dead.
   b. As though he were dead.

10. Which do you say?
    a. I lay down a minute because I was tired.
    b. I laid down a minute because I was tired.

11. Which expression is unacceptable in polite society?

    a. My mom.
    b. My kid brother.
    c. My children.
    d. My kids.
    e. My dad.

12. Which word is unacceptable?
    a. Seemingly.
    b. Irregardless.
    c. Devilishly.
    d. God-awful.

Finished? Now check your answers against the correct

answers at the end of this chapter. If you struck out on any one of these questions, you are a candidate for some tutoring. Any wrong answers on 5 through 12 are proof positive. (Do not feel bad. You have lots of company in the lower echelons, and even a few in higher circles.)

Why One Wrong Answer Can Flunk You

If you wonder how it can be that one wrong answer flunks you, it is because any one of these troubles indicates that you suffer from a wide range of difficulties. Let us analyze some of the wrong answers.

If you answered "yes" to any or all of the questions from 1 to 4, it indicates that cultured or educated speech is foreign to you. You have learned your basic manner of speaking in an entirely different environment, and you will not be able to escape it without help.

Wrong answers to questions 5 through 10 indicate a predisposition toward bad grammar. (The correct answers are *a, b, b, a, b, a.*) Each wrong selection is a common but atrocious error that grates on the educated ear. Unfair as it may be, the automatic reaction of the listener is: If he does not know how to speak correctly, how can he know anything?

Question no. 11 simply applies to habits in different class groups. No upper class member would ever refer to his mother as "my mom." It is just not done. It is as bad as referring to one's mother as "the old lady." Strangely enough, you might get away, on occasion, with jocularly referring to your father as "my old man." (Apparently, fatherhood is not so sacred as motherhood:)

In question no. 12, if you did not spot *irregardless* as the atrocity it is, you need help. The correct form is *regardless.* Where the senseless bastardization came from, heaven only knows, but it marks the user instantly as unlettered.

There you have it. Harsh words, but true. This emphasis has been applied so that you will run, not walk, to the nearest speech clinic or intensive English course.

In addition to good English, the importance of good manners in higher social groups was referred to briefly at the beginning of this treatise. Fortunately, it is not so difficult to learn new habits in this area. The subject is covered in another chapter.

CHAPTER 10

Creating Loyalty In Your Staff

There is plenty of room at the top for those who have the skills and who know how to put themselves across. Like many good jobs along the way, the very top jobs are management jobs; and in a recent ten-year period jobs in management increased by fifty percent, with a total of nine million persons involved. At the same time, capable men for the highest posts have been so scarce, the *Wall Street Journal* has pointed out, that industries are going outside their own organizations to seek executives. All this spells opportunity for the ambitious man, and it is in his interest to give much thought and study to the special skills involved in management, no matter what his field.

We call this the age of computers, but computers will never take over responsible management positions. The competent executive will always be the indispensable man. No machine could ever be aware of the hidden motives, the emotions, the drives, the interplay among the human beings in an organization or a department — factors whose handling makes for the success or failure of an operation.

In this connection, a popular book a few years back pointed out that business has a tendency to promote men beyond their level of competence. A man is a whiz as a salesman, and so he is made sales manager. Knowing nothing about managing men or doing administrative work, he falls flat on his face. A particular artist is promoted to art director in an agency, and has things in a snarl and a running battle within weeks. (In his case his work has been too self-oriented, perhaps, to make him a good manager.) A management engineer who has been used to treating tasks and workers like pawns in his abstract job may find himself completely unable to cope with actual people and all their vagaries.

A basic fact that explains many such failures is that *a leader must have followers.* It is not enough to be labeled *executive.* One must be able to inspire the respect and friendly feelings of those he commands. In addition, the best leaders inspire a measure of loyalty. The people under them are happy in their jobs and put forth their best efforts. When necessary, they will even extend themselves to achieve an unusual aim. Production stays consistently high, and employee turnover is minimal.

Beyond knowledge of your job, beyond administrative ability and organizing genius, this ability to deal with people is of prime importance. It is just another facet of putting yourself across. Here the underlying attitude that comes across to your people is the thing that makes the difference. The verbal approach you use is, of course, vital to conveying your attitude, and key words and phrases are indispensable tools.

Your Role as an Executive

A certain amount of detachment and objectivity is necessary to analyzing the role of the good executive — a role that does not vary greatly, whatever the surroundings. Whether you are running a giant enterprise or a small department, the basic aim is the same. The aim is *production.* Production with economy. Production with profit. Everything that is done must contribute to this ultimate aim, yet the atmosphere should not be frenzied. Workers should be happy; or, at least, content.

The ideal organization should operate as smoothly as a fine machine, each part meshing with the other, each part doing its job without wasted motion, and *without friction.* In achieving this happy state of affairs, good scheduling and proper apportioning of duties are important; but this matter of the attitude and behavior of the manager is perhaps even more important. The parts involved in this machine are people, not metal castings.

Qualities to Strive For

Think over the good and the poor executives that you have known. A composite picture of the good executive, the good manager, will undoubtedly come out something like the following:

- He is a man of dignity and assurance, but without pomposity.
- He is friendly toward his employees, without being chummy. Somewhat of a father figure, approachable, yet quietly authoritative.
- He usually knows his employees' jobs as well as his own, although he may not have the technical skills of some specialists.
- He is fair. He plays no favorites.
- He is sympathetic, in a detached way, but is not overly swayed by sentiment.
- He is tactful, because he is sensitive to the pride and inner feelings of other human beings.
- He knows how to give orders and make them stick, without being a dictator.
- He has a sense of humor and can use it on occasion to relieve tension.

- He can delegate authority without shirking responsibility.

- He is aware of what is going on in his department at any given time. He cannot be fooled by phonies.

- He is a big man, and does not hold grudges, although he demands good work and exemplary behavior from his employees.

- After considering all angles, he can make a decision and stay with it. However, he can admit error or the wisdom of changing course when necessary.

Key Words and Phrases
Important to Getting Results

Measuring up to such a list sounds like a large order, and yet it is not too difficult if you keep checking yourself against the list. Again, we cannot escape the fact that much of the impression you create with your employees depends on the words and phrases that you use. Words project the image, the feeling that you wish to convey. Let us analyze some of the qualities mentioned, and consider some of the key words and phrases that help to create and express these qualities.

The Most Important Words

In the astonishing way of coincidence, I was halfway through the writing of this book, when Luis Cassels, in his *"Washington Window,"* came out with a column touching on the subject of key words. "Eight little words," he said, "could enormously improve the quality of American life."

The words he chose were "sir," "ma'am," "please," "thank you," and "in my opinion." As I see it, the first two words are optional . . . a speaker could just as well use the name of the person addressed, and avoid any possibility of sounding servile or stilted. I heartily agree, however, with Cassels' choice of the other five words, and with his thoughts on them. "Too many people today seem to think courtesy is an optional frill," he wrote. "It's not. It's an essential lubricant of human relations. Without it, friction quickly generates excessive heat."

In my outline for this book I had already jotted down these same six words, under the caption, "The Six Most Important Words." And so they are. If you should develop no other faculty of getting along with people, these six would carry you a long way.

- Please
- Thank you
- In my opinion

Please and *thank you* are such simple words. Most of us were taught them in childhood. Yet an amazing number of seemingly intelligent people neglect to use them, and thus cause themselves needless difficulty every day. This is particularly true in the case of many lower echelon managers and executives.

In order to direct an enterprise, one must give orders; but bald, peremptory orders can become very galling to even the lowliest employee. He already knows that you are the boss, that you must be obeyed if he wishes to keep his job. Why rub it in by omitting the little courtesy of "please?"

Dramatic Effects of Key Words and Phrases

Consider the simplest commands, such as "Come in," and "Sit down." Without the addition of *please* they are the words of a martinet, and the listener bristles warily. With *please* appended they become the gracious request of a gentleman, directed to someone he respects. All this is embodied in the one tiny word; your visitor responds with pleasure and becomes receptive to anything further you may have to say.

An executive must be suffering from a certain poverty of spirit, a lack of confidence in himself, if he feels that he must give bald orders in order to underline his importance.

In doing so he will impress no one but himself, and he will reap a hidden ill-will that may defeat his long-term objectives.

If carelessness or thoughtlessness has led you into this error, resolve now to mend your ways. Pause right now and think up a few orders, with and without *please* appended. Note the difference in the tone.

Please is perhaps the most important of all key words, but the phrase, "Thank you," runs a close second. It has a magic all its own.

Whether you say, "Thank you," regarding compliance with a simple request or to express appreciation for a big job well done, you are conveying many pleasant meanings to your listener. In effect, you are telling the one you thank that you look upon him as an important, respected human being. You are telling him that he has made a contribution that you appreciate. You are even implying, perhaps, that he is a generous human being who has done a little more than grudging duty would have required of him. His reaction to all these complimentary implications is bound to be warm, and he will enjoy his role of being helpful. He will automatically extend himself to earn that thank you time and again.

Other Useful Forms of Request

While we are on the subject of requests to subordinates, let us consider some other approaches and key phrases that are useful. The secret behind each of them is that it indicates your respect and consideration for another human being. Study and practice them in private if you have not been accustomed to using them.

- Can you stop what you are doing a minute, Bill, and come into my office?
- I am sorry to interrupt you, but here is something that will have to be attended to right away.
- I know you are rushed on that job, Bill, but can you stop a minute, please, and look into this?

- Excuse me, Miss Smith, but I need your help on this right away.

- John, can you spare a few minutes, please? This job needs your special touch. (Or) I need your opinion on this.

Most jobs are planned so that employees are consistently busy. To rudely interrupt without referring to this fact gives the impression that you do not know what is going on — or even that you assume the employee is loafing. It also implies that you have no regard for how much work you burden him with, or that you do not think those beneath you deserve consideration. No one who hopes to receive the best efforts of subordinates can afford to incite such rankling impressions. One of the greatest needs of every human being is to feel that he is appreciated, and giving your employee this rewarding feeling costs nothing but a moment's thought.

"In My Opinion . . ."

The last phrase in the Luis Cassels item — "In my opinion" — has not so much to do with handling employees, but is immensely important in your dealings with equals. It is a softening, tactful phrase, that allows you to present a point of disagreement without seeming authoritative or rude. More, and perhaps better, approaches to this problem are discussed in Chapter Six. See "Phrases and Approaches that Make Opponents Receptive."

Techniques and Phrases that Create Loyalty

One of the worst things that can happen to an executive is to fail to achieve the loyalty of his employees. Production is bound to suffer because of low morale. Worse yet, from the manager's personal point of view, his reputation will suffer because of this, and because of the lack of respect reflected in the attitudes and covert remarks of his employees.

From a purely practical standpoint, cultivating loyalty is well worth the effect it requires.

Where shall we start? With friendship, of course. It will be a special kind of friendship, with a certain reserve, but it will be genuine and warm nevertheless. To achieve it you must be interested in your employees as people, and you must present yourself as another human being. You can enter into friendly conversations with individuals and groups. You can briefly discuss their personal problems with individuals when you are invited to do so. You can remember and comment on the big events in their lives.

Since friendship is a two-way street, you can do some confiding also — but keep it to matters that do not concern the business, and to matters that will not hurt your image. Never, whatever you do, criticize your own boss in order to excuse yourself or to ingratiate yourself with employees. In other words, use judgment as to just how much of yourself you will give — without being obvious about it.

When you have arrived at a friendly relationship with your employees, where you have their trust, there will undoubtedly be occasions when some will try to lure you into discussing your own superior. Do not be trapped. Use one of the easy escape phrases in the next paragraph, and change the subject.

Escape Phrases to Memorize

- Yes, he can be difficult at times — but don't forget, he has his problems, too. Let's get on with the job.

- He is in one of his impatient moods. Some problem must have come up.

- Something's got him riled up. Let's see if we can get this stuff out in a hurry for him.

- Well, he's usually a pretty reasonable man. Don't forget, he has some difficult situations to handle, too. Just do your best, and he will probably forget all about this tomorrow.

In all of these you are being agreeable, and yet not joining in the actual criticism. At the same time, you are pouring oil on troubled waters, and giving your employees a lesson in tolerance and understanding. (Underlings sometimes have a tendency to think that all is sweetness and light and a bed of roses in the upper echelons. The idea that the top man may have problems and snafus might never occur to them without your reminder.)

Asking for Help Can Benefit Relations

Dignity and assurance are important to the image of the good executive; yet having an air of assurance does not mean that one should take a know-it-all attitude. As a matter of fact, the executive, especially in creative endeavors, is often more successful with his people if he asks for help occasionally! Remember, people *love* to be asked for help, if they are not actually imposed upon. The following forms of request will bring a warm glow to almost any employee's heart. Make them your own.

- See if you can work out a system for handling these. I'd appreciate all your thoughts.

- I have been mulling over this problem and I am not satisfied with what I've come up with. See what you can do with it.

- I seem to be stymied on this Smith account for the moment. I could use some fresh viewpoints. I'd like to have you take a crack at it. Jot down your thoughts on it, will you please?

- I need your help, Bill. R. J. Greene is coming in at three o'clock to see that presentation, but I've got to attend this Chamber of Commerce luncheon. You know our plans as well as I do. I would like you to drop what you are doing for the next hour or so and jot down an outline. I will let you make the talk when Greene comes in. Just brief me on it when I get back. Here are all the papers. I am glad I have you to depend on.

Note the respect, the expression of confidence that shines

through these requests. They are actual approaches I have heard used by outstanding executives. These men were not softies, yet they were generous with compliments, and their employees worked like slaves to earn them.

How to Turn Down a Suggestion

Of course, after you have gotten your employee's suggestions, it may happen that you cannot use them. You are then faced with the problem of turning them down, which must be delicately handled. You do not wish to imply that he is stupid or incompetent, and you also want to be able to call on his enthusiastic help in the future. Certain key phrases take care of the situation nicely, for instance:

- Well, these are good, Jones. I can see that you have done some real thinking. But they are not exactly what I feel we need. Never mind, though; you have started me thinking, and I believe we can work something out. Thanks very much.

- Thank you, Jones. I may not be able to use any of these in its entirety, but they will enable me to work something out. I certainly appreciate your help.

- Thank you! I knew you would come up with something, Jones. I am going to have to mull these ideas over and see what we can do with them. The situation has changed a little bit, but it may work out.

- Well, these are good. You are getting there. But I would like you to work on it a little more. I want to have several approaches to consider. See if you have any more thoughts between now and next Monday. I am not sure that we have covered the problem of such-and-such, but I want to think about it some more. One of us will come up with the real solution, I am sure. Thank you very much.

In these approaches you make it quite clear that you will not use the ideas, or perhaps not in their entirety. On the other hand you have complimented Jones on the work he has done, and given him the impression that his help is appreciated. He will not be hurt if some other solution is arrived at. He may also come up with more useful ideas himself.

On some occasions you may have to make the man himself reject his own suggestions. You do this by speaking quite frankly.

- Well, I can see you have done some real work on this, Smith; but I don't think you have covered all the bases. What are you going to do about the back-up of material at number seven? That's something that has been stymieing me, too.

In the ensuing discussion, the problem may be fully worked out. If not, just thank the man for his work, and ask him to see you if he happens to come up with an answer. Here you have turned him down, but given him a feeling of partnership which will increase his interest in problem solving.

Using Compliments to Increase Efficiency

All along the line, never be afraid to compliment employees for work well done. Let's face it. Many jobs, like billing or filing that some workers do day after day to earn their daily bread, are boring; yet if the worker feels that he is part of a team and that his contribution is appreciated, he forgets the boring character of the work. He develops pride in his proficiency and extends himself to increase his skill.

If you are not in the habit of complimenting others, make a resolve now to extend at least one compliment to one member of your staff every day. Start noticing people as people and look for opportunities to comment on a job well done. Even one week of your new policy will present dividends that will show up in production figures. Bigger dividends, perhaps, will be the pleasure you yourself reap from the improvement in employee morale.

Phrasing of Compliments

Complimenting others is something of an art, if it is not

to be a mere fruitless "buttering up." Make sure your praise is meaningful, even if brief. Beware also of the backhanded compliment. To simply say, "This is good," or "You did a fine job on this," can sometimes be taken to imply that other work was bad! Remember, you are dealing with people; some of them are ultra-sensitive, and some are harassed with worries and uncertainty that you may know nothing about.

Here are some effective phrasings of compliments. Study them, and jot down some variations of your own, along with some ideas applying particularly to your own employee's tasks.

- I particularly like this, Joe. I think it will more than do the job.
- This is great! All your work is fine, but this is outstanding.
- Keep it up, Bess! You are doing a fine job.
- I think it's great the way you have organized this stuff. You have just about eliminated the bottleneck we had.
- I want to commend you, Bob, on the neat appearance of your department. Perhaps your whole staff deserves some compliments.
- My! You certainly found that promptly, Miss Smith. You must have those files really well organized.

How to Reprimand Without Destroying

Compliments and encouragement, of course, are only part of the picture. In spite of being appreciative when appreciation is deserved, you cannot be an easy mark or a softie. Discipline in general is important, and there are occasions when reprimands are in order. In the latter case, approach with caution. Restrain yourself from flying off the handle, and remember that things are not always as they seem.

When you feel that you must dress someone down, make it a practice to call him into the privacy of your office. This will prevent your embarrassing him in front of others, an

almost unforgivable sin, and it will also give you the opportunity for a calmer approach.

Two things are extremely important in the matter of reprimanding. One is to be sure that you are right, that you
know what you are talking about. The other is to reprimand
without destroying. Keep your perspective, and do not irreparably damage your relationship with a good employee
by inept handling of a situation. The best approach is exploratory. Give the man a chance to present his side of the
question before you land on him with both feet. If you are
too hasty, you may find yourself having to apologize for your
ignorance. Too much of this can undermine respect for your
ability as an executive.

The Exploratory Approach

Here are some examples of good lead-ins you can use
when a reprimand seems in order. They help you get the
facts, so that you can be sure the reprimand is justified.
They will also help you to pinpoint your criticism for maximum effectiveness.

- Please sit down, Bill. I'd like to discuss some things
  with you. *What do you think is wrong in your department?* I suppose you know that you are five
  days behind on the Nelson job.

- Miss Green, I hear there has been some trouble between you and Miss Barrow. Would you like to tell
  me your side of it?

- Jim, I don't know whether you realize it or not, but
  your work has been slipping badly in the last month.
  Can you tell me what you think the trouble is?

- Over the years, Scott, your work has been eminently
  satisfactory, but this last report is really a sloppy job.
  Can you give me any explanation?

- Howard, I like you as a person, and think you have
  the skills for the job you are in, but it seems to me
  you are not measuring up to your abilities. I am going

to give you back this report and let you try it just once more. I will give you until Tuesday. Have you any questions about it?

The Key Word is I

Note that in reprimanding and in settling disputes among employees the key word in your talk is *I. I am surprised...I am perturbed...I have sensed...I should like to hear your side of the matter...I am disturbed about the incidence of such and such...* Such approaches invite discussion and gently lead up to the matter of correction.

Contrast this with the accusatory approach, employing *you:* "You are hard to get along with;" "You are delaying the whole division;" "You have made errors on your last two reports." In these cases you would be passing summary judgment, throwing the person on the defensive immediately, and very likely arousing anger and resentment. At the same time you may be placing yourself in an untenable position from which you may have to retreat.

Settling Disputes Among Employees

Next to reprimanding effectively, settling disputes among employees is probably the most unpleasant task in the executive repertoire — and yet it is extremely important. Employees that are involved in a quarrel or a personal vendetta, no matter how covert, are certainly not producing at full efficiency. Energy and attention are being wasted on extraneous matters. If the situation is allowed to continue, the whole department may soon become involved, with partisanship and gossip generating friction and waste motion all along the line.

Shouting matches are fairly easy to handle, because they are out in the open, but they are quite rare. The personal contests you have to watch out for are the carefully hidden ones that quiet down the instant you come on the scene. A wise executive will never let them fester.

Once you suspect that something of this sort is going on, be alert for additional evidence, and when you are fairly sure there is friction, call the parties into your office to talk things over.

Interview One at a Time

Whatever you do, do not talk to both vendetta participants at the same time. (You certainly do not want to bring matters to a head on your own carpet, with you as referee. No truth will come out of such a situation.) The better plan is to quietly interview the participants one at a time, each out of the hearing of the adversary. Tread cautiously.

Get the Facts

Your object is to get the facts of the matter in contention, and to straighten things out — all in a friendly, fatherly way. Try to be completely fair, especially with women, or you may worsen matters. Once again, the investigative approach is the safest to follow. Here are some tested openings that you should memorize and have ready, should need arise:

- Miss Barret, I seem to sense a little unfriendliness between you and Miss Jones. Is there some difficulty between you? Tell me about it.

- Miss Jones, I was surprised at the sharp way you spoke to Miss Barret. Is there some trouble between you? Tell me about it.

- Carter, I don't like to hear sarcasm between people in the department. Is there some friction between you and Preston? I should like to hear what it is all about. Of course I intend to talk to Preston, also. What's the bone of contention?

- Greenberg, you seem to have been in a rather testy mood for the last few days. What's troubling you? Is there some difficulty in the department?

Occasionally you want to get testimony from a third party before you make your decision in the quarrel. You do not need to judge either party immediately, if the situation is complex. Just say, "I'd like to think about this a little bit.

I'll talk to you again later. In the meantime, I wish you would make a special effort to keep the peace — or to straighten things out. I don't like to see this disruption in the department."

This extended investigation may seem rather tiresome, but experience has shown that it is necessary, even fruitful. There is no better way, for instance, of exposing the fawning gold brick and the goof-off who can keep a whole organization fuming and smouldering with resentment. Moreover, if it becomes known that you are going to look into such situations, hot-tempered types will be constrained to show a little more courtesy, and vendettas will seldom get started.

How to Settle the Matter

After all parties to a quarrel have been interviewed, you will have to settle the matter. Again, do it by speaking to the individuals separately. You might end your judgment with a little talk on teamwork. The same talk could be repeated at a general meeting, to make sure that everyone gets the message. Here are a few "judgment" speeches that can guide you:

- Miss Barret, I have looked into the matter between you and Miss Jones, and I find that you are not filling in the forms completely, which causes difficulties and delays in other sections. If you will remember, when you came here you were told that all forms must be completely filled in. The reason for this is that every item on the list, although it may seem trivial to you, is of vital importance to some other section. I hope that in the future you will be cooperative, and try to follow rules to the letter.

- Miss Jones, I have spoken to Miss Barret about completing the forms, and she promises to do better. If there is any further trouble, let me know. In the meantime I hope you will forget this little quarrel you have been having. I don't like friction in the department. It makes everyone's job harder and cuts down the team's efficiency. If you find you cannot settle a problem pleasantly with another employee, it is better to bring the matter to my attention than to let it fester. Do you think everything is going to be all right now?

- Carter, I have investigated the matter you complained about, and I feel that you are being hypercritical. Preston has been helping out part-time in Department 8 for the last two weeks, you know, because of Smith's absence. If you find he is getting behind here, I wish you would try to give him a hand now and then, instead of getting angry with him. We have to operate as a team, you know, if we expect to keep our record . . . and keeping that record means money in all our pockets. Now that you understand the situation, I hope I can depend on you. I don't like friction in the department.

How to Handle Employee Complaints

Similar techniques to those outlined above can be used when one employee makes a complaint about another. If anything, this sort of situation requires even more investigation, even more coolheadedness, and it cannot ever be swept under the rug. Bear in mind that a problem must usually be pretty bad for any employee to take this drastic step of complaining about another. On the other hand, you cannot assume that his complaint is justified, no matter what your personal feelings are in the matter.

Beware the Gold Brick

To open this discussion, perhaps we should ask, "How does the gold brick get to be a gold brick?" The answer is that he does it by *fooling the boss.* And the reason that he is able to do this is that almost every executive fondly believes that he himself is one executive who is too clever to be fooled. Meanwhile, the gold brick, usually a trusted lieutenant, goes merrily along, infuriating everyone else in the department, but delighting the boss. He is costly in terms of both morale and money.

The best way to guard against harboring a gold brick is to admit to yourself the *possibility* that you could be doing so. Having admitted this, you will make it a policy to check periodically on the actual work record and production record of every key man or woman under you. You will also listen fairly to every complaint that is registered with you, and investigate it impartially.

Do not figure, however, that the gold brick will be the subject of many complaints. He is far too well protected to allow this. Strangely enough, the loudest complainant, the moaner and groaner about his work load, is fairly often Mr. Gold Brick himself. On your climb upward you surely saw him and heard him often. Beware now that he is not pursuing his cushioned destruction in your own bailiwick. If you find him, make him either get to work or leave. If you succeed in the former, he will probably leave anyway, for he does not like work.

Encourage Employees to Make Suggestions

Proper dealing with complaints is just one aspect of being fair. Make sure you are fair in all your dealings with your workers — and that your assistants are fair. Encourage employees to come to you with suggestions about work methods and work distribution. As you go among them, keep your eyes and ears open, and ask questions:

- How is it going?
- Do you think we have the work apportioned in the best way we can?
- Are you getting your material on time?
- Let me know if you can think of a better way to do things. I am always interested in improving the system.

When the noted Edward E. Carlson became president of

United Airlines, he spent considerable time traversing United's thousands of miles just to talk to employees. Hearing from stewardesses that one New York hotel treated them like second class citizens, he switched their New York headquarters to the Waldorf Astoria. Stewardess morale soared. His direct contacts led to many other beneficial changes that would not have occurred if he had relied on the usual channels through many-layered management. For instance, a stewardess told him that United had upped the price of beer from fifty cents to one dollar a bottle, and she thought it was ridiculous. He agreed and put the price back at fifty cents . . . an inexpensive way to improve customer relations.

His tactful explanation to the stewardess when he countermanded the price rise is worth noting. "Someone got overzealous and made a bad decision," he said.

How to Stress Teamwork for Loyalty and Results

Asking for suggestions, showing interest in each man's work, builds up the individual's sense of worth, his dedication to you, and to the team if you have laid sufficient emphasis on teamwork. In order to do this, you yourself must think of the department or the organization as a team, and explain the concept thoroughly to your people.

At nearly every meeting, make it a point to demonstrate with charts and facts and figures your own section's place in the big picture of the organization, so that your people can know what they are working toward. Take time out frequently to explain the workings of your own department as a team. Show how each individual job meshes with the others. In addition, you may wish to occasionally set departmental quotas, with a prize to the division or the individual who sets the best record.

Do a Little Bragging in Public

Another great way to develop pride in the department as a team is to do a little bragging in public, when the opportunity presents itself. Key phrases like those that follow can be extremely productive. Your people are really impressed by confidence expressed publicly.

- We can depend on my people to help out.
- I have a great team here. Every man does his part.
- I am proud of our record of efficiency. There have been some snarls in the past (or some errors), but with the help of everybody we have gotten them straightened out, and I think we are going to see a vast improvement from here on out.
- If a prize were given for efficiency, I think my people would win it.

How to Phrase Effective Pep Talks

The same technique is a clue to the phrasing of effective pep talks. Lambasting and blaming people when sales figures or production figures slide is rarely productive. The resentment aroused paralyzes action. It is much better to ask for cooperation in solving the problem, giving praise for past successes. Here are some examples:

- I have called you people together this morning to ask for your help in solving a problem. As you know, business conditions in general are bad, but I feel that our own figures are not quite as good as we could make them if we faced up to the challenge. I have been proud of the way you have surmounted difficulties in the past, so let us put our heads together and see if we can think of solutions now.
- It is my belief that there is a solution to every problem, and I think that among us we have an excellent collection of good minds. Let us analyze this situation, work on it, and get those graph lines swinging upward again. Right now! Who has a suggestion?
- I think you three gentlemen probably know why I have called you together this morning. I have been somewhat perturbed at the declining figures in your

divisions, and I want to get your thoughts on the situation. This is a rather new thing, to find part of the organization lagging, and I know you are as interested as I am in finding the answers. I have confidence that if we analyze the causes properly we can remedy them. You men have always produced in the past, and I know you can do it now. Let's look at the charts and discuss the matter.

CHAPTER 11

How to Achieve a Successful Telephone Personality

If someone should ask you, "Do you know how to use the telephone?" your startled reply would almost certainly be, "Of course I do!" We grow up with the telephone, and it is so much a part of our lives that we automatically assume that we know how to use it. We rarely think of it as an instrument that needs special techniques of handling; yet many a career has been made or broken on the telephone.

Consider for a moment. You may be the embodiment of grace and charm in person, with a handsome face and an engaging smile, yet you have none of these things going for you on the telephone. Your whole image, all your subtleties of meaning, must be conveyed by your voice alone and the words you choose. This is true with your friends, but even more so with strangers.

When you are talking face to face, a harsh or ill-chosen phrase may pass unnoticed because of the warm smile or the pat on the shoulder that accompanies it. In case it does not pass unnoticed, you are constantly studying your listener's face, and you automatically attempt to correct any wrong impression that you see registered there. The advent of the picture-phone may bring some part of this advantage to the telephone, but even a picture cannot bring all the warmth of a personal encounter. Communicating by telephone, especially in business, will still remain a particular problem that needs study by anyone interested in successful encounter.

I am not referring to telephone-selling or anything of the sort. I am speaking of the ordinary day-to-day use of the telephone in business and personal affairs. You can make the telephone a barrier to success or a distinct aid, according to the way you use it. If successful telephoning is not your forte, start now to make this much-used instrument your ally. There are definite rules for going about it.

The Basic Attitude to Cultivate

Of the utmost importance to your success on the telephone is your basic attitude. Any hint of arrogance or imperiousness comes through devastatingly. It is much easier for the party at the other end of the line to react uncooperatively, or even rudely, than it is for the same person to do so face-to-face. He can even cut you off, more or less at will. Knowing this, it is your job in a telephone call *to create the reception your words will be given.* To a large extent, a good basic attitude accomplishes this feat. Your attitude sets the scene, as it were. (The telephone company had this in mind when they used "the voice with a smile" as their advertising slogan for so many years.)

"That's all very well," you say, "but I may be talking to a stranger or to someone with whom I have never hit it off." Granted. Nevertheless, a good basic attitude is your best guarantee of winning over the stranger or securing the cooperation of an unpleasant personality. The No. 1 rule is to project warm friendliness, no matter who it is that you are addressing.

My own method of achieving this productive attitude, and

one that is used by most successful people, is to always take the point of view that I am talking to a good friend, a respected friend, whose cooperation, helpfulness, and goodwill I can always expect. Be he janitor or corporation president, the approach is always the same, with infinitesimal variations or none at all. It works miracles in creating warmth and receptiveness at the other end of the line.

Proven Methods of Achieving a Good Attitude

This warm attitude is something you can start using immediately, even if you have to conjure up a friend's face to help you in the beginning. Before you pick up the telephone, next time and every time, whether to answer a call or to make one, say to yourself:

- "Ah! This is my friend, of whom I am very fond, and he will surely do his best to make things easier for me."

Write this magic phrase on a card and keep it in your desk drawer, so that you can take it out and read it before you approach the telephone. Its power will prove a revelation to you, and very soon the attitude it creates will become second nature.

I knew a man once in a newspaper advertising office who went even further in his effort to put warmth in his approach. He always answered the telephone with, "Hello. This is Bob Richards. What can I do to help you?" Perhaps he carried things a little too far; and yet it was amazingly effective, both in setting *his own* mood and that of his listener. His skill on the telephone may well have tipped the balance in his favor when there came an opening for the post of advertising manager.

One man in the same organization who wanted the job very much was a capable, conscientious fellow, but he had an uncontrollable temper which occasionally boiled over on the telephone. Time and again Bob Richards or the publisher himself was called upon to straighten out an emotional mess created by this man. The poor fellow became embittered and even shorter tempered when he was passed over and Bob Richards was made advertising manager. Soon afterward he left the paper to try another field.

This is an extreme case, yet thousands of men and women create needless problems for themselves and their companies by the wrong approach and the wrong words on the telephone.

Important Telephone Words

After schooling yourself in the right attitude and practicing it until it becomes second nature, your choice of words is almost guaranteed to be good; yet it is important to remember a few indispensable words and phrases.

As in almost every business situation, the most important words to always remember are those prime key words, "Please," and "Thank you."

If you think this is too obvious to be stressed, start listening critically to some telephone conversations around you — perhaps even your own. I have observed disastrous results many times from the omission of these words of basic courtesy.

A Bad Telephone Call

I took on a new advertising assistant once, in a small store, who almost wrecked the department with her terrible telephone manners. One of her chief sins was the omission of "Please" and "Thank you."

In the high-speed, high-pressure business of retail advertising, one must have the friendship of everyone concerned, from errand boys to printers and buyers, to top executives, if the work is to click out on schedule. Since much contacting is done over the telephone, skill and finesse in the use of this instrument are unusually important.

Shortly after my new assistant had started to work, some ad proofs came in that had to be checked and o.k.'d by the buyers immediately. (They embodied a last-minute change.)

Barbara (not her name) was assigned to call the buyers and ask them to come up to the department to do the checking. Now, buyers are executives, heads of departments, and are often quite irascible types, because of the risks and the pressures of their work. By and large, they must be given tender loving care at all times.

Barbara, like many young people, was quite puffed up with the importance of her new job. To my horror, I heard her telephone a particularly difficult buyer-personality in a crisp, thoroughly "businesslike" voice, as she saw it. "Mr. Hellion," she said, "this is the Advertising Department. We want you to come up immediately to o.k. some proofs."

There was the sound of an explosion on the other end of the line, and Barbara flushed and put down the phone. "He says I'll have to bring them down," the girl said meekly.

Here, in the midst of an already impossible rush, Barbara had gratuitously presented us with an additional time-consuming problem. We did not have the personnel to run proofs to individuals. There was also the matter of creating a dangerous precedent with a demanding personality like Mr. Hellion.

After our minor crisis was past, and it was one of many, I took Barbara in hand once again for schooling in successful telephone technique.

Successful Methods That Win the Listener's Co-operation

First of all, the so-called "business-like" manner or tone has practically no place in modern business — and it certainly has no place in the success-oriented person's bag of equipment. The successful ploy in almost every encounter, as has been stressed, is to create as much friendly feeling, as much cooperativeness as possible in your listener.

What Barbara should have done was:

1. Although Mr. Hellion was a natural-born "antagonist," in spite of being a gifted buyer, Barbara should have completely dismissed this image from

her thoughts before approaching the telephone. In preparation, she should have said to herself, "Mr. Hellion, I know you are a busy, very important person, but you are my good friend and I like you, and I know that you will do everything you can to help me."

2. Her remarks should have anticipated her "opponent's" objections — sweetly, sympathetically, thus throwing him off-guard.

3. The request should have been phrased in such a way that the listener would find it almost impossible to refuse.

4. Those key words that never wear out — *Please* and *Thank you* — should never have been omitted.

5. The young woman should have taken her listener into her confidence, asked his help.

6. If possible, she should have mentioned an advantage to the listener.

An Example of Correct Techniques

Correctly staged and phrased, the telephone conversation to the difficult buyer should have gone something like this:

"Hello! Mr. Hellion? This is Barbara in the Advertising Department. We've got a terrific problem up here. You know those ads that Mr. X changed at the last minute this morning? Well, the proofs just came in, and Mike is waiting here to take them back. (Or, perhaps, the paper has given us one-half hour to get them back.) We know you are terribly busy down there, but could you please take a minute to come up and o.k. your ad? We want to be sure the prices and colors on your merchandise are right. I have to call everybody."

Even self-important, quarrelsome Mr. Hellion could scarcely refuse this request. I know from experience that he would not have, even if he were furious at being forced to cooperate. He should then have received the sweetest of thanks: "Oh, thank you so much. I've got to rush now. Goodbye."

Here we have it. Let us analyze in detail that seemingly artless telephone call. (Great art always makes its point without emphasizing the fact that it is art!)

First of all, in this approach, the manner and language are *casual,* not "business-like." The whole thing has a friendly, intimate warmth to it, without any embellishment or compliments. It sounds like a telephone call from a friend.

Two. The friend presents a problem that needs the listener's help for solution. The problem is explained briefly, in words the listener can surely understand, having himself experienced Mr. X's impetuous ways.

Three. The listener's expected objection, "I'm too busy," is anticipated, and thus circumvented, in a most sympathetic tone. By her brief reference the caller is saying, in effect, "I know you have problems. You've told me about them, and I have listened, and I understand." This is something she could never say in so many words, of course, but a prickly character like Mr. Hellion is actually dying for sympathy and understanding. He usually sees himself as a martyr, and a crumb of sympathy has a tendency to soften his attitude. (A word of caution is needed here, however. You must go on quickly to your own situation and request, or this type of listener may sidetrack you by going into his troubles at length.)

Four. In the example we are analyzing, the listener is enticed into becoming emotionally involved in the caller's problem by the reference to Mr. X's vagaries, from which all have suffered. The caller is saying, in effect, "We are in the same boat, and we must work together to save ourselves. You know how it is."

Five. The caller clinches the request by a clear reference to the listener's own self-interest; i.e., "We want your ad to be correct, because you are our friend, and we know that you will want to help us get it right."

Six. With "I have to rush!" the caller comes back to the problem at hand, emphasizing her own predicament, in which she needs help, and excusing a hasty "Goodbye" that cuts off argument.

Plan In Order to Get Results

This is the complex reasoning and planning behind a seemingly spontaneous call. With good planning, the intended result will be obtained ninety-nine times out of a hundred. In the case of an actual Mr. Hellion, you must be prepared also to sweetly suggest alternate solutions. If he still refuses to come to the department, the caller might say, "Well, could you send your assistant, please? We must have an o.k., and the boy is waiting." As a last resort, one might say, "Well, I guess we could break the rule this one time. I'll read you the ad, and maybe you can give me your o.k. over the telephone."

Fortunately for all of us, personalities as difficult as Mr. Hellion are rare. Yet, unless your telephone technique is a good one, you can actually create difficulties with the most normal and the mildest of listeners.

The underlying principles are the same for every telephone call, almost without exception. Summarizing, you might add these pointers to your reminder card:

- Plan my talk.
- Don't forget:
    Please
    Thank you
    Goodbye

Always Say "Goodbye"

An amazing number of people sometimes forget to say goodbye when finishing a telephone call. The results of this can often be disastrous, especially when the person you have been talking to has been angry. Even in ordinary conversation a person may jump to the conclusion that you have hung up on him, and the fat will be in the fire. Never risk such a situation. Engrave on your mind the importance of saying goodbye on *every* occasion before you hang up the phone.

Handling the Angry Caller

These rules of being friendly and courteous never vary. You are almost never permitted the luxury of becoming angry on the telephone. Even if the caller happens to be angry or critical, you should not let yourself be shocked out of your own friendly approach, or your CONVICTION that the caller wants to be pleasant, wants to be helpful. In ninety-nine times out of a hundred, your attitude will calm down the angry caller and permit a rational solution to the problem that is upsetting him. If he does not calm down immediately under your friendly handling, remember the old admonition; agree with thine adversary quickly. The following phrases should be memorized for such possible occasions:

- *I don't blame you for being angry, Bob.* I know how important this project is to you. Give me a couple of minutes, and I'll see what I can do to straighten things out. I'll call you back inside of ten minutes. *Goodbye for the moment.*
- *I don't blame you for being upset, Joe.* It's obvious that someone goofed. *What do you think we should do to make amends?* Just tell me, and I will see that it is done.

The last procedure applies when there is no apparent solution to the problem an error has created. In using it, you may think you will be laying yourself open to outrageous requests, but it does not work this way. Most people are so taken aback by your generous offer that they backtrack. Their anger departs and they begin to minimize the error, to see it in perspective. In my experience, if they make any request for amends, it is usually less than you would have expected, or been willing to do. If it should be out of bounds, you can usually think of an alternative solution that will be readily accepted. (Here again, by your manner and your words, you are assuring the man you are talking to that you know he is a reasonable, friendly person. He will strive to measure up.)

How to Make a Complaint on the Telephone

When you yourself have to make a complaint over the telephone, it is a good idea to remind yourself of what the purpose of your call is. The purpose, in practically all cases, is to have the error corrected as quickly as possible.

A secondary purpose is to maintain good relations. If you find your own temper getting the better of you, get out your reminder card on basic telephone technique. Force yourself to take the friendly, productive approach. This is particularly important if the company or person you must call is a valuable link in your business; but it is worthwhile in any case. No matter how firm you must be, make your approach friendly and understanding, and you will find that the matter will be taken care of much more efficiently at both ends of the line.

The following are some helpful approaches to implant in your mind for such occasions. All of them have been used by experts. Note the touch of humor here and there.

- Bill? Joe Green here. You know that parts index you sent us? Well, I hate to tell you, but we have checked and re-checked it, and there seem to be several errors in it.

- Bill? I know how busy you fellows are down there, but you have gotten us into a kind of mess here. We still have not received the missing charts for the Aero job. What can you do about it? Neither you nor we can afford to miss that deadline.

- Bill, you are a nice fellow, and I like you, but I am thinking of crossing you off my list. Where the devil is that shipment you promised would be here last Thursday?

- Mr. Brown? This is Joe Green of Staples & Company. Ordinarily I wouldn't trouble you about a thing like this, but there seems to be some kind of communications breakdown lately. I decided that I had better ask for your help.

- Bill, I don't mean to be making a complaint about Mike. He is a very efficient fellow, and a good friend of ours; however, I don't seem to be able to reach him, and something has come up that has got to be attended to immediately. Can you help?

Admit Your Own Error Quickly

When the shoe is on the other foot, and you, not the other fellow, are at fault, learn to admit your error quickly and make amends. No good can come of trying to cover up or shift the blame. You will find that when you do admit your error (assuming you are not in the habit of erring), your adversary will be far easier on you than if you had tried to dodge responsibility (see Chapter Eight).

How to Turn Down a
Telephone Request Tactfully

During the early years of World War II, when business was still very bad in many fields outside of Defense, I had a prosperous little display business of my own in New York. Ridiculous as it seems now, there was a printer who used to pester me for work. I had nothing to do with printing during that interval, and yet this man must have called on me three or four times in order to secure a little order for business cards. He was the soul of courtesy and thanked me profusely for the order. So much for that.

Years later I was in a much bigger business and needed to have a couple of thousand posters printed. I happened to think of my "friend," and so I gave him a call and inquired if he were interested in the job. To my utter amazement, one of the rudest voices I have ever heard crackled over the wire. "No!" the man said. "We're not interested in any little job like that. "We're in Defense business."

There was no point in my keeping the peace with such a character, and so I let him have it. "Listen, you pipsqueak," I told him. "I gave you a job once out of kindness when you were starving. The least you owe me is courtesy. Etc., etc." He stammered and made an attempt at apology, but nothing could undo the damage he had done.

I do not recommend my technique in this instance, although New York is filled with cooperative printers and I did myself no harm. The little story is told to illustrate how stupid it is to make a rude reply to any customer's inquiry over the telephone — any request, for that matter. Courtesy is easy to practice, and it makes everyone's life so much pleasanter. Many times it even pays off in money dividends. How did this man know that I might not have a giant rotary press job to give out, in addition to the posters? (As a matter of fact, I did handle such printing.)

Some Well-Phrased Turn-Downs

A simple reply, like, "No, I'm sorry, we don't do posters," would have been sufficiently courteous in the above case. Here are some better replies that create goodwill and friendliness, and may even bring in some future business. You can adapt them to your own firm's picture. The key words are *"I'm sorry,"* indicating that you regret not being able to be of service.

- No, I'm sorry, but we are not equipped to do posters. We are geared for giant runs, and if we took your job it would actually cost you extra money. I suggest you call a silk screen outfit.

   (To be given a helpful steer is greatly appreciated by the caller. If he is given an actual name to try he will be even more grateful, as . . . "Why don't you call Green & Company? I think they handle this sort of work.")

- No, I am sorry, but we cannot handle your work at this time. We are just swamped with Government contracts, and we won't have any presses free for six months.

- No. I'm sorry, but we specialize in snap-out forms. We don't do general printing any more. Why don't you call Green & Company? Ask for Mr. Blake. If he can't do the job, I'm sure he can tell you who might do it for you. I have his number right here, if you'd like to have it — 454-9870. Later on, if you have any invoices or other forms to be printed, we should be very happy to serve you.

If your switchboard operator or your salesmen answer telephone inquiries, train them in this technique of being helpful. It pays off in good feeling and good business.

Other Tactful Refusals

The same general theory applies to refusing any request. Being courteous and attempting to be helpful is especially important if you are talking to someone with whom you work constantly. Make sure you leave your caller with the feeling that you would LIKE to help him if you could. Here are some phrasings you can adapt:

- Gosh, I'm sorry, Bill. I'd love to do it for you, but I'm catching a plane for Chicago in twenty minutes. (Or, I'm due at the main office for a big meeting in ten minutes, and it is going to keep me all afternoon.) I sure hope you can work things out.

- Bill, I'd like to help you out, but I am so swamped with work I don't think I'll ever be finished with it. Of course, if you weren't in such a rush, I might be able to sandwich it in some time next week. Do you think you could possibly work it that way?

Notice the concern and the interest expressed in these replies. A similar line is used if you must refuse to be imposed upon by a good customer who is making an unjustified complaint. In these cases, try to present a compromise, if possible, as suggested in the last two of the examples that follow. In the end, if you have to, it would be better to accede to the customer's demand, no matter how unreasonable, rather than lose a valuable account. Be extremely careful that no hint of annoyance or anger enters your voice. And remember, nothing makes an unreasonable man angrier than to be told that is is being unreasonable.

- Gosh, I'm sorry, Joe, that this thing has caused such a commotion — but that's the way the order read. Maybe in the future we should double-check these orders with you before we proceed. Do you think so?

- What a mess! I can't tell you how sorry I am, Joe, that this thing happened. In the future I am going to check and double-check before we make any change in your schedule. I wish you would mark all your stuff to my attention hereafter. I am going to personally supervise your account from here on out.

- I'm sorry, Arnold, but I can't possibly give you the old price on this order. Our costs have gone up all the way along the line, and it would put us out of business if the word got out. I know you understand that. Besides, B. J. would have my scalp. Why don't I come over and talk to you? Maybe we can figure some way to cut costs elsewhere in your operation.

- How about if I write to your customer and explain the situation?

- (If you must compromise.) Well, you are really putting me through the wringer, Arnold; but I know you wouldn't do this unless you were forced to. Let me talk to B. J. and I'll call you back. He will want to help if he can. (Here you give yourself time to work out the least costly solution to the demand.)

- You know I want to help you, Arnold. We have always been friends. Let me figure a minute here. How about if I send you back the order and you make it an addition to your last order? It's a risky thing to do, but maybe I can slip it through.

- Gad, I'm sorry about this mess, Arnold; but maybe there is a way we can work it out. Could you beef up your order? If you could use 50,000, even if you have to buy ahead, I could give you the quantity discount. That would come within a few dollars of the old price. See, the break comes at 50,000.

Manners Toward Frequent Contacts

In all your telephone conversations, try to adopt the informal quality of the telephone conversations given in this chapter. Again, the big point is that if you speak as a friend, there is every chance that you will be treated as a friend.

In the case of someone you must contact frequently on the phone, but never see, go even further. Make it a point to remember some of the personal facts about him and his life that happen to be revealed in the course of your acquaintance. Inquire about his health, his kids, just as you would if you were talking to a man in your office.

CHAPTER 12

How to Write Letters That
Do The Job Gracefully

Most Honored Sir:

Your esteemed favor of the 15th instant received and contents duly noted. We beg to advise that said order was shipped March 10 last by oxcart, in the care of one James Parsons, who is on his way to Philadelphia, and you should be in receipt of same in good time. As per your instructions, it is our pleasure to enclose a copy of invoice herewith.

Assuring you of our humble appreciation of your patronage,

I beg to remain,
Your Obedient Servant,

Jno. N. Carlton

The handcut quill pens that wrote such letters in another day have long since disappeared, along with the obsequious closing. Yet, strangely, quite a few of the timeworn phrases still survive in modern letters.

Many otherwise intelligent, well-informed people still approach letter-writing as though it were a matter of translating ordinary English into the archaic forms of oxcart days. Laboriously they search the mind for trite, obscure expressions, and rob their letters of all sincerity and force.

The Key to the Modern Persuasive Approach

If you have been guilty of including even one old phrase in your correspondence, stop now and take a modern approach. Letters, after all, are for communication. As nearly as possible, a letter should use the same words, the same manner you would use if you were speaking to the addressee face to face. To write, "Yours of the 16th instant received and contents noted," is just as ridiculous (and dull) as it would be to say this in person to someone you were thanking for a birthday card.

Avoid these Trite Phrases

Beg to Advise — Do not beg anything; and advise only when you are actually giving advice.

Enclosed please find — Will it really be necessary to search? Say instead, *Enclosed is* or *I am enclosing.*

As per — Use *per* only in per cent, per diem, per annum, and such Latin terms.

I have before me — A silly and superfluous introduction to a letter of reply. Just get on with what you have to say.

Contents noted — Another senseless superfluity.

Thank you for your favor of the 10th — If you mean letter or order, say *letter* or *order.* The same goes for *check* or *payment.*

Herewith and *Hereto* — More unnecessary appendages, often used redundantly. Eliminate them.

Wish to say — Never mind the wishing. Just say it.

In re — In the body of a letter, say *regarding,* in *reference to, expanding on,* or whatever it is that you really mean to say.

Same — *Same* is an adjective, not a pronoun. Instead of saying *we will ship same,* say *we will ship the merchandise, the chairs,* or whatever it is you intend to ship.

With this one step, eliminating the trite, you will put yourself well on the road to more effective letter-writing. The following two letters about the same situation illustrate the point.

First the dull, trite letter:

> Dear sir:
>
> I have before me your favor of March 14 and wish to say that the merchandise was only now received by us. Same will be shipped by air freight, as per your instructions, at an early date. Enclosed herewith please find copy of invoice. We appreciate your patronage.
>
> Yours very truly,
>
> J. S. Oldtimer

The well-written, modern letter:

> Dear sir:
>
> I am happy to tell you that your order of March 5 will be shipped by air freight tomorrow, and should reach you in plenty of time for your sale.
>
> As you know, the longshoremen's strike has caused some delay of shipment to us, but luckily the Japanese freighter that has been at anchor here for a week was unloaded yesterday.
>
> I went back to the shipping room this morning and personally supervised the selection of your merchandise. It is being packed now, and a copy of the invoice is enclosed.

Please let me know if there is anything further we can do to help with the plans for your Anniversary Sale. You have all our best wishes.

Yours very truly,

Joe Alert

Why This Letter is Good

The second letter is longer, but not too long, considering the definite information it gives, and the reassurance. In all likelihood, it was far easier to dictate the longer letter than the more obscure short one.

Joe Alert's letter illustrates several important principles of good letter writing.

A clue: See if you can decide to whom it was that Joe Alert's letter was written. Outside of the formal "Dear sir" and "Yours very truly," it might have been addressed to "Dear Ed," a lifelong friend of Joe's. With few exceptions, good letters are like that. They carry an element of warmth and personal concern. The writer comes through as a person — a person who gets up off his chair and does things, who remembers you as a person and is interested in your problems. He does not talk gobbledygook. He speaks plain English and tells you in so many friendly words what it is that you want to know.

Mastering the technique is not difficult. Just close your eyes for a minute before you start to dictate and get a mental picture of the man to whom you are writing. Think over his letter and what it is that he wants to know. Then answer him, just as though you were talking face to face, keeping in mind the key words and phrases that fit the situation. Do not try to impress with your importance or your vocabulary. Just write as you would speak to a friend that you know very well, concentrating on making your message clear.

Get to the Point
You Wish to Express

Usually it is not necessary to summarize the letter to which you are replying. The man knows what he wrote. Just answer him as though you were talking to him, avoiding any old-fashioned, stilted opening.

Bad	Well-Written
Replying to your letter of August 4 in which you inquire about the durability of our product, I wish to say that all our products are warranted to give satisfaction.	I am enclosing a copy of the warranty that accompanies our XL carpeting. As you can see, XL Carpet is expressly made for the high-traffic areas you have in mind.

Occasionally, of course, it may be necessary to mention the letter to which you are replying. In this case, do it gracefully and briefly and get on with your message.

Bad	Well-Written
I have before me your favor of January 14, and I wish to say that we are embarrassed by the delay in making a reply. The truth of the matter is that your letter was sent to the wrong department and has only now come to my attention.	I have an apology to make. Your letter of January 14 was somehow mislaid and has only now come to my desk. I hasten to send you the price lists you requested and some swatches that I believe are suitable to your needs. I hope that we are not too late with this material, but I suppose these things are bound to happen now and then in every organization.
If you are still interested in the price lists and swatches requested in your communication, please inform me and I will send them at the earliest possible date. In future please address all communications to me personally to avoid delays.	Please forgive us. And rest assured that your account will be given special attention from here on out. I have sent out instructions that in the future every letter from you be placed on my desk immediately.

The letter on the left is not only badly written, but it embodies a snide attempt to blame the customer for the delay. This is not unusual in such situations, but it certainly does the company no good. If the writer had been speaking simple English, he might have recognized his error. Even the most gauche in public relations would scarcely say, "We are sorry, but it was your own fault."

The writer of the first bad letter quoted, J. S. Oldtimer, has fallen into a similar trap. Although he probably did not intend it, there is a feeling of impatience, even annoyance, in his letter. Stilted language is likely to engender this sort of impression.

Every Letter Carries Two Messages

No matter what sort of person you actually are, and no matter what you are writing about, every letter you send out over your signature is going to carry two messages. One will be the message you intend. The other will be a message about *you*. The quality of the stationery, whether it is engraved or printed, well or badly designed, will give some idea of the importance of your job. The appearance of the letter and the quality of the typing will tell something of how much you demand from your employees. More than these, the tone and the general feeling of the letter will give the reader a definite impression of you as a personality.

Because of this hidden message, every letter presents an opportunity to promote yourself and the company you work for. Take advantage of this fact by making sure that you put yourself across as the pleasant, intelligent, and efficient executive that you really aim at being.

Never Write an Angry Letter

One should be particularly careful never to let ill-feeling creep into a letter. Although the mails are swift, there is still a time lapse, and great harm can be done before you can attempt to counteract it. For another thing, remarks that are written and formalized may be read again and again, and may become over-emphasized.

If you suspect that anger or even irritation has crept into your letter, do not send it. Save it and read it over when you are in a calmer mood.

On the occasions when you must differ with someone, be careful to do it with tact. Review the chapter on how to differ winningly, and make particular note of the key words and phrases.

Some Good Models for Difficult Letters

Note the positive, even flattering introductions used in these letters, and the leisurely, thoughtful pace of the wording. You can adapt these models to many uses.

Dear Jones,

I find your letter and the drawings on the Parsons project very interesting. Your plan has considerable merit, but before you make a final decision I should like to present a few thoughts of mine, for what they are worth. All are open to discussion, of course.

1. Are you sure the J & L steel suggested is quite strong enough? I am thinking maybe we ought to prepare from the start for heavy manufacturing use that may develop later. The added cost would not be prohibitive, would it? If so, could we absorb it somewhere else — perhaps eliminating some of the frills? I wish you would look into this angle and let me know what you come up with.

2. Several years ago, I remember that the Delacourt outfit ran into difficulty with water seepage from underground streams. This was about two miles south of the Parsons site, but it is something to keep in mind. I suppose you have checked it out.

3. I should like to see at least another hundred square feet given to the shipping department — again contemplating future use. Don't ask me where you are going to find the space. Perhaps you can chisel it off the lobby and the back offices.

I hope you won't think me carping. In the main, you have done an impressive job, overcoming some difficult problems. Please telephone me if you have any questions. I know you are pressed for time.

With very best personal regards,

George Reynolds

This letter illustrates the importance of keeping in mind the point of view and the *feelings* of the person to whom you are writing. Reynolds could have written, "The plans as you have drawn them up won't do. For one thing, the shipping department is too small, etc." The letter would have been briefer, but the aftermath could have been most lengthy.

Use of Key Phrases to Soften Criticism

Before he began his letter, George Reynolds obviously had thought of Jones, an expert in his field, who had done a great deal of work and presented it with some pride. Reynolds' problem was to suggest necessary changes, without hurting or angering Jones, so that they could proceed on friendly terms. He used key phrases liberally:

- Your plan has considerable merit.
- Before you make a final decision.
  (These two phrases are a gentle way of re-opening a subject for discussion. You just assume that the plan was not intended to be final, and go on from there. This gives the author of the plan a face-saving out, if his "baby" has to be rejected.)
- For what they may be worth. (In other words, "Your opinion is valued, also. I am not setting myself up as an inflexible expert.")
- I am thinking again . . . (Again softening the criticism. The question form also helps.)
- I suppose you have checked it out. (Expresses con-

fidence, yet enables Reynolds to give an important reminder. Jones, if he was remiss, can easily say, "Thank you for reminding me of the trouble the Delacourt outfit ran into downstream. We are having tests made right now.")

- Don't ask me where you are going to find it. (A casual way of saying, "I know I am giving you a nasty problem, but I have confidence you can solve it.")

Brevity is Not Always a Virtue

In writing important letters, do not get hung up on copybook rules. Brevity is to be desired, in general, but you should never sacrifice tact and good personal relations to brevity. In the letter above, Reynolds, although not especially brief, made his points very clear by the device of tabulating them.

Short sentences may also have to go by the board in the interest of diplomacy. In the first paragraph of Reynolds' letter there could have been a semicolon or a period after *considerable merit.* However, this would have made the break too obvious, especially if he had used a period. Reynolds wanted Jones to slide right into his trap, without noticing the device. Clarity is not sacrificed.

Follow Up If Necessary

When Jones reads Reynolds' letter, if he has any intelligence, he will realize that changes have to be made in his plans. He will doubtless go ahead and make them, or at least discuss them. If he does not, of course, Reynolds will have to follow up his tactful letter with definite instructions to do as he says. In that case, he might have to speak rather bluntly, but still graciously, as:

Dear Jones,

I am sorry you did not completely approve of my suggestions, but I have discussed the drawings with the principals, and they brought up the same points. It seems we are going to have to make the changes.

1. — —
2. — —
3. — —

Please send me the revised plans as soon as you can get them in order.

Again, I want to thank you for all the work you have put into this project. I think it is going to be a tremendous success, and I am sure it will bring you some additional laurels.

Yours very truly,

George Reynolds

How to Turn Down a Request and Keep a Friend

Letters turning down a request have to be delicately handled if good will is to be retained. Here are some examples that can be useful as models:

Dear Mr. Peterson:

I am honored that you should ask me to speak at your next general meeting, and I wish I could come. However, the situation here has gotten so involved, with two of our key men out, that I do not feel that I can leave, even for a short time. I know you will understand.

I hope you will not have too much trouble lining up another speaker. Have you considered Harley Masterson?

With the thought that they may be of some use, I am sending you under separate cover a copy of an article I wrote on the subject. I have also included some of the research material I gathered. You may want to use some of these things in displays.

Please let me know how things work out. I can't tell you how sorry I am that I cannot join you.

Cordially yours,

Joseph Krausmeier

Tactful Key Phrases

Kindly, but without beating around the bush, Krausmeier lets his correspondent know immediately that he cannot accede to the request. He follows up with some effort to be helpful. The whole letter has a warm, appreciative sound. These are some of the key phrases:

- I am honored.
- I wish that I could.
- I know you will understand.
- Let me know how things work out.

Some other requests can be even more difficult to turn down, but it can be done gracefully if you can think of convincing reasons for refusing. Here is an example:

Dear Ben,

I appreciate your thinking of me in connection with your new venture, but I am afraid I cannot come in with you. Right now I have my modest capital invested in so many things that it is all I can do to give them the minimum of attention. At the same time I am actually strapped for surplus cash, and market conditions do not warrant liquidating any holdings.

Even though I cannot join you, Ben, I want to wish you the best of luck. You really deserve a break.

With warmest regards,

Henry

Some of the material in this letter may be white lies, but they are justified. It is not necessary to tell Ben the bald truth. He can gather Henry's opinion of his venture from the definite negative that runs through the kind letter. Henry dared not intimate any enthusiasm at all for the proposition, lest he invite further pressure.

If his opinion of the project had been asked, he might

have said: "I looked over your material with some interest, but was not too impressed with the possibilities. Of course, I am not an expert in this field — and that is just one more reason for me to stay out of it. I hope you will understand."

Do Not Be a Slave to Dictation

If dictating letters is difficult for you, or if there is a particularly troublesome letter among those on your desk, do not be a slave to dictating. Take the time and write out your reply, or at least outline the points you want to make, before you call in your secretary. You can even explain to her, if you wish, with "This next letter is extremely important, and so I have made some notes." You will not lose face with her. She will appreciate your wish to be accurate in the first draft.

CHAPTER 13

Making The Formal
Presentation Your
Big Opportunity

If, in some magical situation, the ambitious man were told that he might have one wish granted, he might say, "Give me a chance to show how much I know, how thorough I am, how good I am at organizing, how well I get along with people, how skillfully I manage people!"

The wish sounds like a mouthful, and yet all this and more could be granted in one single opportunity — the opportunity to make a formal presentation. If such a chance comes your way, do not shy away from it. Seize it eagerly as a ready-made situation in which to spotlight yourself and all your abilities.

The project will be a tremendous challenge, of course, but careful planning and strict attention to the key words and phrases can almost guarantee that you will carry it off successfully.

Formulating a Dramatic Plan
— The Structure

Whether you are going to present an idea, a system, or a piece of machinery, the first step is to *write down your objective,* and then to plan the structure of your presentation so as to reach this objective in the most compelling way.

Writing down your objective is done for the purpose of clarifying it in your own mind. To begin with, you might write, "My object is to demonstrate this new piece of machinery." But IS this your object? Aren't you really going to try to show how this new piece of machinery will save labor, save time, and cut costs in the company? That is a better statement of the objective.

Now plan the structure of your presentation to bring home that objective, step by step. The most usual way of doing this is to proceed in logical order, working to a climax near the end. This may be the best way in a specific case, but again, it may not be. There is another method, technically called *in medias res,* that often works out much better. Consider both approaches, before you decide.

In medias res is a Latin phrase that simply means "in the middle of things." In presenting items in which there is a quantity of dreary detail that must be covered, this approach is often superior. It gives you a plan with two climaxes, as it were — one at the beginning and one at or near the end. The necessary details can be sandwiched in between.

Suppose, when it was brand new, you were going to make a presentation of an electronic oven to people who knew little of electronics. If you tried to "start at the beginning" and explain to them the structure of the oven and the electronic devices within, you would lose them right off the bat.

The proper technique would be to employ a dramatic beginning, demonstrating the use of the oven, and then, if necessary, go into the structural details.

You might start out with the rather startling announcement, "Ladies and gentlemen, I have here a pan of brownie batter that Miss Clark has just mixed for me. As you can see, it is just regular brownie batter. (Demonstrate.) While we are talking I thought I would bake us a batch of brownies, so that you can be sure you will enjoy yourselves. Would you believe they are going to be ready to eat in six minutes? Here. I'll set the timer on my magic oven for exactly six minutes. There we are!

And now, while the brownies cook, I am going to tell you something about the amazing things this new electronic oven will do for your business . . . "

The same approach would probably be best with almost any great improvement in machinery. Take, for instance, the electric mimeograph machine that uses electronic stencils, and turns out work that compares favorably with printing. Anything like this benefits from a demonstration that starts your presentation off with excitement. Sometimes, if the machine itself cannot be shown, you can use movies, or just show the product of the machine and discuss its superiority before you go into the mechanical details.

Write Your Plan in Detail

When you have decided which beginning to use, write out in detail your entire plan for the talk and the demonstration. Fit everything to the interests, the intelligence, and the capabilities of your audience.

In addition to the plan, and keyed into it, write down all the visual aids and illustrations that will be needed. Ask for help, or hire help if possible, to take care of necessary artwork. If such help is not available, keep to what you can do on your own. If you cannot draw, prepare to use the item itself to illustrate your points, or possibly plan on using photos or photostatic blow-ups. Any graphic illustration should be kept simple, colorful, and easy to understand. You might plan, too, on some items that will be handed out for the audience to examine.

The amount of research you can do and the length of your presentation will both be guided by time factors. Make sure to stay well within your time limits, to avoid any sense of urgency or pressure.

Write Out Your Speech
and Anticipate Questions

After you have done the planning and arranged for all the props and the art that will be necessary, write out your speech just as you intend to give it. (Perhaps thorough notes will do, if you are an accomplished speaker.) In any case, organize your speech in every detail. Also think of any questions that may be asked, and write down the answers to them.

In formulating your talk, make sure that everything you say leads step by step to your objective. Keep the speech logical and natural. Above all, make sure that you do not present yourself as a pompous know-it-all. As you write, picture the attitude you wish to convey. The friend bringing good news; the helper with problems; the money-saver; the bringer of a new tool *your listeners* can use to advantage — these are usually good attitudes to project.

Remember that speaking to an audience, even public speaking, has come a long way from the days of the spellbinders and silver-tongued orators. Audiences are different; outlooks are different. Part of the change in attitude is due to the fact that most "public" speakers — presidents, senators, generals, foreign leaders — now come right into the living room via TV. The ringing phrases of the past are toned down to an intimate, person-to-person quality.

Use a Tape Recorder for Practice

The tape recorder is an invaluable aid to speech-writing. As soon as you have your talk written, record it and play it back. When you do so, you can tell immediately what spots are weak, where language is difficult to speak, where tediousness creeps in. Make your changes and try recording again, until you are satisfied.

Show That You
LIKE Your Audience

Your speech should have much of the quality of conversation. To begin with, you must *like* your audience, and think of them as liking you. Whether or not you will use a microphone, speak as you would speak to a group of friends to whom you want to tell something that will be interesting and important *to them*.

Write your speech with this sense of *liking* firmly in mind. When you deliver the talk, maintain this attitude. Keep smiling; keep your feeling of happiness, enthusiasm, and good humor. This is especially important if there are interruptions or skeptical questions.

Setting the Stage
for Smooth Performance

If possible, get to the place where you are going to give your speech ahead of time, and see that everything is in order. Take a checklist with you to make sure nothing is overlooked. Arrange your props, your visuals and charts. Check the adjustment of the microphone, if any, or test the amount of voice projection you will need to reach the back rows. Check the heating or the air conditioning. Last but not least, make sure you have your notes on hand. (It is a good idea to carry a duplicate set in your inside pocket.)

When movies or slides are to be used in connection with your talk, try to arrange ahead of time to have an operator manage these. Supply him with a small light to prevent fumbling, and instruct him thoroughly as to how you will cue him in. (If in the end something does go wrong, just take care of it matter-of-factly and in good humor.)

Beginning the Show — the
Person to Person Approach

If you cannot arrange your props and equipment beforehand, do it quickly and deliberately after you have been introduced, explaining casually what you are doing. You might say, "I'll just take a minute to get everything arranged, so I can tell you this story the way it should be told."

When you finish the preparations, you could say, "Now we're all set up here. How about you people? Would you like to have the air conditioning turned up? And can everybody see? Why don't you move up closer — fill in these front seats." This is the person-to-person approach again, and helps establish rapport. Be flexible. (When preparing your speech, make sure that the introduction fits in with such proceedings if they should become necessary. Anticipate, so that nothing will throw you.)

It is a good idea to ask that questions be reserved till the end of the talk. You might say, "Before I begin, I want to say that I know you are going to have lots of questions, because I am going to tell you about something brand new and extremely interesting. If you can, I should like you to save your questions until the end. Just jot them down, and I will try to answer everybody. Of course, if we get to a point where *I have not made something clear,* raise your hand, and I will try to straighten that out right away. NOW! Let's get the show on the road." (Begin presentation.)

Key Words and Phrases are
Vital to Persuasion

Note that you do not say, "If you don't understand . . . " You turn the idea around and use one of the key phrases for such situations:

- . . . where I have not made something clear.
- If I have not made myself clear.
- If I have not explained well.
- If I have not covered everything.
- If I have left something out.

You put the burden on yourself, not your audience. (See Chapter Seven.)

All the way through your talk and especially in response to questions, the key words and phrases will be extremely important to keep your audience's interest and good will. Hold the thought throughout that you are a friend, talking to friends; never show annoyance. If someone criticizes you or your product, turn the criticism to your own benefit. One of these key phrases for reply will help you to state your message:

- I am glad you brought that up, so I can clarify things.

- Thank you for pointing that out. I can see that I haven't explained it as well as I should have. Now here is something I didn't mention ... or I didn't dwell on enough . . ..

- You're right. I should have taken that into consideration. Here's the thing I should have brought out . . ..

- You're right, but I am having a little difficulty explaining the working of this. I wonder if you would come up and help me hold this, and perhaps I can show how the automatic control works. Come on. I'll wait for you.

Taming the Hecklers

The last phrase is an extreme device for controlling the baiter or the relentless heckler. Once you get him up on the platform with you and give him something to hold, he is usually paralyzed. Such a man rarely counts on being spotlighted, and when he is, he is usually overcome with stage fright and embarrassment. On the rare occasions when he is still unruly, tell him quietly and sweetly that you will see him in your office later and go over the whole thing with him — but do not let him leave the platform until he is thoroughly humiliated. If you can, give him something to hold that puts a little strain on him, and forget about him for a few minutes. When he is ready to collapse, rescue him with great solicitude, and let him go back to his seat.

Occasionally you may have to agree with the interrupter, without making it seem important, and go on to something else. The following phrases are useful:

- That's probably true; but I want to get on to this other big advantage.

- We'll go back to your question later. I am sure the two of us can work it out. But right now I want to show you *this*. (Turn to a new angle, or go back to one already discussed and elaborate.)

- Yes, you have a point there, maybe. But *this* is really what I want to emphasize — and that's *the money* it will save you, the time it will save you. I am sure you will be a wizard at using this thing.

Throughout the whole presentation, talk about your audience in relation to your subject, and not about yourself, except incidentally. If you demonstrate an item, be sure to say, "Think what you could do with this, with all your skill!" Then give examples.

Be Considerate of Your Audience, and Help Your Cause

Sometimes, if a presentation is a long one or highly technical, you may note that your audience is getting tired, or you yourself may be tired. In such cases, either summarize quickly or create a break in which people can get up and move around. Here are some devices that can be useful:

- You have all probably been curious about the exhibits that are posted around the walls. I suggest we take a short break now, so that you can go up and examine them. Afterward, I'll ask for questions. (Or, I'll demonstrate some of the other wonders that can be produced by this machine.)

- I think we are all getting a little tired. I suggest we take a short break and have some of the refreshments that are waiting in the back room. I'll bang the gavel at the end of ten minutes, so I can show you some of the other ways you can save money with this machine.

- I suggest we break for lunch now and meet here again at two o'clock. There is a lot more you will want to see in this exhibit. I believe it is going to revolutionize our business.

Coming to a Successful Conclusion

In the original preparation of your formal presentation, give yourself a choice of conclusions, so you will not be at a loss when you near the end of your talk. In deciding which ending to use, feel your way and note your audience's reactions. If the audience seems completely sold, drive on to the signing-up stage, the voting stage, the money-paying stage, or whatever is appropriate. Key phrases like the following tie up the package:

- Well, gentlemen, I see that you are as enthusiastic as I am about the possibilities here. Let's take a vote. All those who think Brown & Company should install these new machines please raise your hands.

- Well, sir, I think we should go about planning the installation, don't you? What about next week?

- I am going to have some cards passed out now, and if you will sign them and note your company's address, I will go ahead and arrange for the thirty days' free trial.

For another occasion, when you feel that you might not have altogether made your point or completed a selling job, be prepared with an alternate conclusion that does not demand a final decision. Leave yourself a second chance. Phrases like these are useful:

- Gentlemen, now that you have seen this remarkable machine, I am sure you will think of a dozen ways in which it can save your company money. After you have had a chance to discuss it with others in your organization, I will be in touch with you. In the meantime, call me if you would like another demonstration or if there are any questions.

- I won't ask you to make a decision on this tonight. I am sure you will want to discuss the changeover with others in your organization. I want you to know that I will be very happy to help you with the presentation.

Just call me and we will make a date. Better still, fill in the card that you found on your seat and drop it in the box at the door. Thank you. It has been a pleasure talking to you, and I shall look forward to seeing you again soon.

• Let's not make a decision on this today. Let's sleep on it and study the ways it can be used; then I suggest we take it up again at next week's meeting. (Or submit it to the entire board, perhaps.)

Keep Something in Reserve

As a final word on successful presentations, you will find that the experts never tell quite all. They always keep a little information in reserve as grist for another meeting or material for conversation. It might be a history of experience with the item. It might be the story of some scientific tests, data on comparisons with other machines — anything of interest. It gives you a good feeling and more assurance if you know you have ammunition on hand for another round.

Incidentally, keeping something back will also save you from making the weak closing one sometimes hears: *Well, I guess that's all. That's the story!* This is a negative closing that lets everything ravel out. Avoid it. You want to leave the impression that there is a great deal more that could be said, while you use a closing that invites action or decision.

CHAPTER 14

Social Situations with The Boss—How to Make Them Pay Off

Like many crucial situations in a career, the occasion when you can be with the top executive socially is a two-headed monster. Depending on the way you handle it, it can lead you on to glory or it can cast you back to the lower depths. Even if you think of yourself as most competent socially, there are special angles to be considered. The wisest course is not to chance being thrown by surprise, but to plan ahead. Long before any such occasion arises, think over every contingency and be prepared with the right words, the right moves. You and your wife should both read this chapter and discuss it at length, since your wife may also be involved.

Social situations in and around the work base are no problem. You are on guard then, and more or less in charge of the situation. It is when the locale changes and new elements enter the picture that danger threatens.

When the Boss Treats You
to Lunch or Dinner

It is fairly simple to handle things when the boss takes you to lunch or dinner by yourself, whether he is alone or with friends. Only table manners and general demeanor will be important. You can probably order anything you like, because it will doubtless go on the expense account. If he does happen to be a skinflint type, you can look over the menu and then ask him what he suggests, or what he is going to have. This will give you an idea of what you are expected to do. In the matter of behavior, keep your drinks at a minimum, no matter what your host does. (You want your mind to be at its best.) A drink before dinner will be fine; but if the old man goes bar-hopping after dinner, you will be wise to stick to beer, or even cokes. Do not try to impress the bartenders. The boss is the man you must keep in focus.

Old Conversational Taboos
Always Hold

The old taboos against religion and politics as conversational topics were probably originated by businessmen. Stay away from these areas, unless you are absolutely sure that you and the boss see eye to eye. Even then, you should change the subject as quickly as possible. There is too much thin ice. Get back to the safe ground of business or sports, or your superior's hobby.

Games to Play and Not to
Play With the Boss

Games are for fun, but many people get extremely serious about them. If your boss is a very competitive type, think twice before you accept his invitation to join him in a game in which you will endanger his standing. Sports that involve one individual against another are relatively safe, because it does not matter if you are beaten — and you can help the other man to win, if it seems wise. Team sports are fine, too, if the boss' team is somewhere in the middle, or if you are a competent player. If you are a dub, don't be cajoled into messing up the team's winning record. Fix some ironclad excuses in your mind now, so you will have them ready when you need them. Choose any of the following key phrases to avoid engagements:

- I wish I could help you out, but we are giving a dinner party tonight, and I have to be there.
- Gosh, I'd love to play, but we are signed up for bridge tonight and I can't back out.
- I wish I could, but my mother just arrived from Kansas City, and I haven't seen her yet.
- I wish I could, but I am to speak at a club banquet tonight. There's just no way to get out of it.
- I couldn't do a thing for you, Bill. I sprained my shoulder heaving some boxes around last night, and it's killing me. You wouldn't want me, anyway — I am a lousy player.

You might add the bit about being a lousy player to any of the excuses, to ward off later invitations. If it is true, you can also say that you do not know a thing about the game. (If it is not true, don't say it and risk being found out later.) Note that in every case, when you beg off, you make it clear that you are sorry.

Games that are quite safe to join in include pool or billiards, Monopoly, Scrabble, Rummy, and similar games. These can engender comradeship and good feeling. Again, you can somewhat control the outcome, if it becomes necessary. The same points apply to sports like golf, tennis, handball, or volleyball.

Some Card Games Are Poison to Careers

Never, whatever you have to say to get out of it, agree to fill in as the boss' partner at Bridge. Even if you have twenty masterpoints to your name — or perhaps because you have — you cannot possibly win, as far as your career goes. There are just too many systems and conventions involved, and a bridge player can hate you forever if he feels that you crossed him up. (Study the list of excuses given above.)

Poker is another game that is risky in regard to good relationships. If the stakes are high, there is too much tension involved. (If you lose, you probably cannot afford it. If you win, you will not be loved.) On the other hand, even if stakes are low, the inevitable drinking may lead to trouble.

Bringing the Boss Home to Dinner

In many a career, there are times when one practically has to invite the boss home for dinner. Such an occasion can be a wonderful opportunity to solidify a friendship, if it is handled properly. Make sure you and your wife think about this situation ahead of time, talk about it, and plan for it. This way neither one of you will be flustered when the day comes.

No matter how good a housekeeper your wife is, or how good a manager, never bring home such an important guest without letting your wife know about it ahead of time. Make your spur-of-the-moment invitation *tentative* until you can call your wife, then hasten to a private telephone. If some disaster has wrecked the household schedule, you will find out about it and can easily switch the invitation to a restaurant meal. (Your credit cards come in handy here.) On the other hand, if all is in order, your wife can proceed with the plan you have already formulated during the present discussion.

Your plan for entertaining the boss at home should cover the food that will be served, what you will do with the children — all crucial details.

Experienced hostesses in such situations recommend that the simplest food be served — simplest to prepare, that is. A standard meal should be kept in mind for such an occasion. An ideal one would consist of baked potatoes, roast beef, one or two frozen vegetables, and sliced tomatoes or a simple salad. None of these require any fussing and they are foods favored by men. If dessert is to be served, let it be fruit or something that is on hand. Wine can be served or not, depending on whether it is in the pantry. The main thing for wives to remember is to keep things simple, and above all, never to experiment with new or fancy dishes. Take no chances.

Steak, incidentally, is something the experts say should be avoided in almost any impromptu menu. Cooking it just right is too tricky, and then it must be served the moment it is ready. It is better by far to rely on good, medium rare roast beef, and avoid any short-order items that will put a strain on the cook and hostess.

The children? In a servantless household (and most are nowadays), your wife can get them cleaned up while the roast beef and potatoes are cooking. If possible, she should line up a baby-sitter to take care of the small ones right after dinner. By this plan you can show off your youngsters at mealtime, then have the evening free for adult conversation or entertainment. The baby-sitter can put the children to bed, read to them, or do whatever is necessary.

A special word about children is called for here. If they are dining with you and the boss, or the boss and his wife, let the children eat in peace — or not eat, if they prefer it that way. A social occasion is no time to be correcting or scolding your children, as many people do. I have been a guest at some family meals where the evening was completely ruined because all attention — and unpleasant attention — was given to the host's children. If you feel that the children are not behaving well, ignore it, or be as quiet and brief as you can about mending the situation. It never impresses anyone favorably to see a big man bullying a little child. If nothing worse, it gives evidence of lack of poise on the man's part — or the woman's, if she is the culprit.

When the Boss and His Wife Both Come

When both the boss and his wife are coming to your home for dinner, the same simple food arrangements are recommended. The big issue to be considered in this case is the matter of how the two ladies will get along, and how your relationship with the boss may be complicated. You and your wife should discuss such an eventuality ahead of time.

One thing a conscientious wife will want to avoid is any possibility of upstaging the boss' wife. Your wife's clothes should be simple and smart, but not flashy; and makeup should be kept fairly conservative. In conversation you should both be yourselves, but strictly observe the taboos on religion and politics as topics. If arguments develop, and they may, keep in mind your key words and phrases. End the dispute as soon as you can — even by agreeing, if necessary. The following key phrases are good ones to keep in mind for such delicate situations:

- That's an interesting viewpoint. It had not occurred to me before.
- You've almost persuaded me. I'll have to do some thinking about it.
- I believe we are closer together in our thinking than we realize. Both of us agree that this is the case . . .
- I got sort of carried away there. I want to apologize. The fact of the matter is that I agree with almost everything you have said. Let's forget it. How about a game of Scrabble? Are you a Scrabble fan?
- Let's forget about the politics and have some fun. We agree on all the main things. How would you like to play some Monopoly? My wife is a whiz at it!

**The Barbecue is Good
for Home Entertaining**

In the summertime, the outdoor barbecue presents a solution to many entertainment problems. The informality is welcome, and does away with the question of what wives and youngsters should wear. In the matter of food, simplicity is again the key. You may find it easier to have a fowl or a roast on the spit than to bother with steaks and hamburgers on the important occasion when the boss and his wife are guests.

Going With Your Wife
to the Boss' House

When you are taking your wife to your boss' house, whether for dinner or just for the evening, there is one factor you must consider if you want your wife to be comfortable and happy, and thus at her best. That is the matter of clothes. Make sure you get the information that will tell her what to wear. To women, the proper clothes are extremely important to their feelings about themselves and to the impression they make on other women. Get the information for her.

When the boss extends the invitation, say frankly, "My wife will certainly ask me what she should wear. Will there be other guests? Should she wear a dinner dress?" If he does not know, ask if your wife may call his wife to find out. This is better than leaving matters to chance and having your wife appear in a pantsuit when others are in formal dress — or vice versa.

Correct Behavior Toward
Your Spouse is Important

When wives enter the picture, a new factor enters your relationship with your superior. Make sure that your behavior is such that it betters your career prospects. If you and your mate are one of those couples who spend all their time cutting each other down, you will be wise to eliminate these tactics when in important company. Such behavior is boring and embarrassing to others at any time, but it can be fatal to the impression you make with the boss and his influential partner. Even joking put-downs are out of order.

The attitude that pays off is one of unobtrusive but loving consideration and respect for each other. When you go in to dinner, you should help your hostess with her chair, and then help your wife with hers. If you observe little niceties like holding doors and lighting cigarettes for ladies, be sure you include your wife in these polite services. Not to do so will mark you as a boor.

In conversation, be guided by your host and hostess, but avoid the dangerous topics in any case. If the talk turns to children, no matter how wonderful your kids are, be careful never to top your hosts' stories about theirs.

When I had a gift shop some years ago, I lost a good customer by being absent-minded on this last point. He was telling me how his eighteen-month-old daughter had developed a trick of ordering everyone out of the room, and then sitting in lonely splendor. "Oh yes," I said, thoughtlessly, "that was the age when my daughter used to slam the door and yell, 'Privacy!'"

My customer gave me a look of fury and disbelief, placed his selections on the counter, turned, and left the store! He never returned.

Manners and Proper Etiquette
Do a Selling Job

So great a part of making a good impression depends on good manners and proper social procedure that you and your wife would be wise to invest in a good etiquette manual. To many people it is extremely important that your reply to a written invitation be correctly phrased and on the right sort of paper, for instance. In the case of wedding invitations, whether you are sending them or replying to one, it can be ruinous to depart from tradition. All such things and much more are covered briefly and clearly in the social arbiters' books. If you are not sure on every point, refer to the authorities. It pays in the impression of yourself it conveys.

Occasionally you and your wife may be invited to a restaurant dinner party or to the theater. Here again small details of etiquette are important. Remember, for example, that the ladies precede the men in following the head waiter to the table, and that the hostess leads the way. When you are dining and foods unfamiliar to you are served, it is all right to comment on this, if you feel you must; but eat them, anyhow. Watch your host and hostess for proper procedure, and maintain your poise.

On theater and restaurant dates, clothes will again be important to the impression you and your wife make. Be sure to inquire ahead of time as to what should be worn. This does not mean, of course, that you should go out and invest in new wardrobes. There is no use in trying to impress the boss with extravagance on any social occasion. He knows how much money you make, and foolish spending could give the wrong impression.

The most important thing about any social situation is to enjoy yourself, and to make sure that others do. That is why you should prepare yourself ahead of time with the knowledge and the skills that are needed so you can be completely at ease, make the best impression.

CHAPTER 15

Successful Direct Selling —
of Yourself or Your Product

Chapter 15 is headed "Direct Selling" to distinguish it from the subject that has filled most of this book — the ongoing process of *indirectly* selling one's self, which occupies most of us during all the days of our lives. Here we will look analytically at the matter of selling a product or a service at a price, and go into some of the key approaches, the key words and phrases that apply. We will also look briefly at the business of selling one's self for a job. (In these situations the person himself is the product the salesman is presenting.)

Study Your Customer and His
Needs Before You Begin

The first step in all successful selling is to be prepared with some knowledge of your customer so that you can fit your sales talk to his needs, his interests. No one is going to buy anything unless he is sure it is going to serve his particular needs, whether practical or emotional. That is a truism, and yet is often overlooked.

When I have been an advertising manager, I have been simply astounded at the amount of their own time and the amount of the prospective customer's time that ill-prepared salesmen will waste. Salesmen from some radio stations were glaring offenders. On more than one occasion, these earnest men would insist on seeing me, and then absolutely demand that I listen to a recording (played through a dummy radio) of programs they had prepared for our store.

The whole approach was fantastically inept in the case of a store that had its own advertising department.

Here were these men, with absolutely no training in retail advertising, no knowledge of the store's policy or its inner workings, spending the station's time and money to record meaningless blurbs. They then attempted to sell this canned garbage to an expert copywriter and an advertising manager who had to make every budget-penny count. Worse yet, the salesmen never learned anything when their goodies were turned down. They were completely defeated and usually quite furious. They could not understand why they were received so coolly, why their brain children failed to charm. Most of them did not even wait to hear the reasons for the turn-down. They were convinced that the customer was stupid or had no funds, and they were anxious to be off to the next victim.

We did buy radio time frequently; but never from these salesmen. Note the difference. We bought radio TIME, then filled it with our own copy — with wording that our experience told us would bring the customers in.

Ask Questions

If you do not know your prospect's needs, his viewpoints, his motivation, it is rarely indeed that you can sell him. In cases where you cannot find out these things in any other way, ask the prospect. The radio salesmen's canned blurb approach might have worked for a mom and pop store, but never for a department store. What these salesmen should have done was come in with a price appeal and a questioning, exploratory approach like the following. (The price appeal interests anybody.)

- Mr. Ad Manager, station XX has a wonderful buy right now on some one-minute spots in prime time. We think you could use them to advantage during your Easter sales. You could write the message, or we could do it for you. Either way, we know you could increase your sales.

  Here's a chart showing what the hardware store down the street has gained by using these spots. Etc., etc. *If you used these prime spots, would you want to write the copy in your department, or would you want our script writer to do it?* We would be glad to write it, and there would be no charge.

At this point, with this approach, an exchange of ideas would be engendered; the salesman would know whether or not he should introduce his recorded broadcast. He would know, too, what he should do to clinch the sale — if budget money was available.

Some basic principles are illustrated by this story. Jot them down and refer to them before you embark on any sales campaign.

1. Do not assume that you know your customer's business, unless you have studied it.

2. If you cannot get the background on the customer, take an approach that will appeal to anyone. *Key phrases* in this category are:

   - Here is a wonderful buy. (Tell why.)
   - This will increase your business. (Prove it.)

3. Show respect for your customer. Assume that he knows his needs, knows his job. (Of course, you may skillfully work to increase his needs, or make him see needs he never knew he had.)

4. Ask questions to get the information you must

have to make a sensible and effective approach. (In the model situation above, this is done by offering the customer a choice of methods to consider. The customer would get involved in discussion and volunteer necessary information.)

5. Don't do a one-shot selling job, staking everything on one approach. Leave yourself an opening for a second chance. *Key phrases* that may keep the lines open when all seems lost include these:

   - We have some other package offers from time to time that are very interesting. I'll give you a ring the next time something big comes up. May I?

   - When you have more time I'd like to work out a program suited to your needs. Can we get together and discuss it next week? How about Thursday?

   - I'd like to tell you about some of the other things we are planning for stores next season. Why don't I take you to lunch one day next week, and we could go over it? How about Wednesday? What's a good day?

   - I know so much more about what your needs are now, I'd like to go back and work on this. I have some other material that I am sure would interest you. May I see you again next Thursday? What day would be better?

6. Don't blame the customer for your failure. Analyze what you might have done (and what you should do next time) to keep the interview or the connection alive. Be flexible.

You Must Sell Yourself as Well as Your Product

Some salesmen come on like pitchmen, even like bullies; but these are nearly always fast buck artists, one-time Charlies.

The salesmen who make reputations for their companies, and build big earnings for themselves, demonstrate that selling one's self is basic to doing really well with the product.

This process is subtle. It consists mainly of presenting one's self as a friend, a helper. The salesmen's words may vary, but his *attitude* says:

- I have something I must show you, because it will help you. Or it will cut costs, save you money. Or it will speed up production.

In some fields, of course, the powerful appeals of love, pride, attractiveness, and status are involved in the help the salesman offers.

- I have something I must show you because it will bring out your beauty, make your skin lovely, make you more appealing to the opposite sex . . . etc.

  It will make your children healthier, or more successful in school. It will make your husband healthier, or happier, or more successful.

  It will make your house a showplace, or make you a community leader.

You cannot sell any of these ideas, of course, unless you can lead your customer to welcome you, believe you, have faith in you. The key words and phrases we have discussed in other chapters are indispensable aids in accomplishing these ends. For special problems there are other key phrases.

Don't Knock Competing Products
— What to Do

If your customer is already sold on a competing product, do not knock it. To do so is to insult him, to tell him his judgment is bad. Use his liking for the other product as a basis for building up your own product. For example:

- Yes, that's a good product, but we have added two extra ingredients that make ours amazingly more effective. I'd like you to try it.

- Yes, that's a good product, but I think you will find that we have gone beyond them in engineering. They demand tolerances of only 1/1000th of an inch. We demand 1/10,000th — and that makes a difference in the speed and in the life of the machine. Note the guarantee that we give you . . .

- Yes, that's a very effective product, but we have managed to make ours just as effective — and we have eliminated some of the toxic features in the older compounds. Let me show you this biochemist's report . . .

Don't Bring Up Negative Factors — But Have the Answers

Occasionally your product is trickier to handle, increases labor costs, or has some other drawback. You do not have to bring up such drawbacks. You sell the positive qualities. However, do not underestimate your prospect's intelligence, and do not attempt to lead him astray — if you hope to continue to sell him. Figure out ahead of time what you will say if he should bring up the negative factors. Here are some phrases you can adapt to your own needs:

- That's true. But experience has shown that our product will increase your production to a level that will more than take care of the slight extra cost.

- We haven't heard of anyone's having trouble with the unions over this, but if there should be some question, I believe you can handle it easily. Cutting costs like this will expand your operation. I think you can show the union representatives that you will soon be hiring far more men than now. There will just be a brief adjustment period.

- It's true, there might be a little more breakage with the glass containers, but we have found that the compound holds up better when it is packed in glass. The plastic seems to make it deteriorate.

Don't Oversell, Don't Pester

You have to learn to sense the moment when your customer is sold, and get him to sign on the dotted line. If you go beyond that point and keep talking, you may start him to thinking about something that will turn him off. On another occasion, if you have talked and talked and don't seem to be getting anywhere, end the interview pleasantly, before there is an actual turndown. In doing this you make it possible to try again another day, when moods and conditions may be different.

Whatever you do, when the selling is difficult, do not make a pest of yourself. Do not call back too soon, and do not call back at all unless you have something interesting to say — some additional information, a new idea on what the product can do for the prospect.

It is even possible after a sale is made to destroy the connection and cut off future dealings by making a nuisance of yourself. I had an astounding experience with this sort of thing, which can serve as a horrible example.

This also happened when I was a retail advertising manager. (Ad managers are magnets for salesmen.) In this instance, a leading fashion magazine presented a promotion idea that I fell for right away. It had tremendous possibilities, and there seemed no reason not to tie in with them on the promotion. All the store was required to do was put a small sign in a display window, saying "Top-notch Magazine has designated Blank & Company as the Top Fashion Store of San Diego." In addition we were to print this phrase in our ads at fairly frequent intervals.

In return for this mention of them, the magazine would list us on a page in every issue, calling attention to the fact that we had been selected as the top fashion store of our city. Great! We were delighted to comply with this little exchange of backscratching — especially since we were not the best store in town nor the biggest.

There were no strings attached to the magazine's offer, but

the woman who was promoting the tie-ups seemed to have a personal axe to grind, or perhaps she was just a congenital pest. First she wanted tear sheets of the ads bearing the promotion phrase, and that was agreeable. It is fairly simple to get and send tear sheets. Next, however, she began to demand photographs of our windows with the sign in them, and this is a quite expensive and time-consuming matter. I wrote and told her that if the photographs were going to be required, we would rather not be in the promotion.

Out of the blue three days later, I got a telephone call from Phoenix, Arizona. Having no contacts in Phoenix, I was mystified, but I accepted the call. It was from Dottie Brazen (not her name), of Topnotch Magazine. "How are things going?" she wanted to know. "What do you think of the tie-up with Topnotch? Are you getting comments from your customers?"

I told her I thought the program was fine, but that we could not go to the expense and trouble of getting our windows photographed for her. "Didn't you get my letter?" I asked.

"Yes, I got your letter," she replied, "and I was very happy to hear that you are getting such good response to the program. Your comments were very interesting. Topnotch Magazine is delighted to be associated with your store."

"But . . . Miss Brazen . . . that isn't what I wrote you about . . . "

"Oh yes!" she said. "We're getting the same wonderful reaction from all our stores! Well, goodbye. It's been nice talking to you." With that, Miss Brazen hung up.

A week or so later I got another letter from her requesting photographs. No mention was made of my letter or the telephone call. I ignored the request.

Two days later I got a call from Lake Placid — with the same idiot exchange of conversation! Two days, three days, a week apart, there followed literally dozens of such calls — from Sun Valley, San Francisco, Miami, Asheville, Hollywood! It was unbelievable. After the first couple of calls

I refused to accept any more, or to call back when I found a message on my desk to call Dottie Brazen. That did no good; I just received another call.

I sat down and dictated an unequivocal blast to Miss Brazen, withdrawing from the program and telling the woman to remove our name from her list. This accomplished nothing. The calls kept coming, until I finally went over and threatened to murder the switchboard operator if she put another call through. I told her to tell Miss Brazen that we were no longer interested in the promotion, and that I would not accept any more calls.

Ten days or so later I breathed a sigh of relief and my secretary and I laughed to think that we were finally rid of my long distance caller. Too soon, alas.

In the midst of our glee the president of the store appeared, wild-eyed and distraught, in my doorway. "Mrs. Cresci!" he cried, as the phone rang. "Please take that call and rescue me from that Brazen woman! In a weak moment I agreed to talk to her once, and now she is calling me every day!"

I took the call, and I forgot all the key words and phrases that apply to getting along with people. I finally had to tell Miss Brazen that if she called me or anyone else in the store one more time I would be forced to get in touch with the publisher of her magazine.

"I'm glad you are so pleased with our program," she replied. "We're getting the same reports from all our stores. Thank you so much. Goodbye-ee!" I think I let out a scream, but it turned out I had finally gotten through to Miss Brazen, and we never heard from her again. Just lately I noticed that Dorsey's, across town, has now been selected as the happy top fashion store!

Of course, nobody but a slick (and perhaps slightly demented) New Yorker would pull such a brazen stunt. The unfortunate thing for Miss Brazen in our case was that she was dealing with an ex-Manhattanite, who could divine her purpose. The moral of the story is, "Do not pester your contacts out of existence."

Legitimate Follow-up Pays Off

Legitimate follow-up is another matter. If you have established a really friendly connection with your customer, you can often come back just to have coffee together, or to take the prospect out to lunch. By doing so you remind him of your existence, and you may be able to put in a plug for your product that will eventually pay off. It is better, of course, if you have something new to say, some additional selling point to bring up.

Techniques of Selling
Yourself for a Job

All that has been said about selling a product applies in some measure to the matter of selling yourself for a job. This is particularly true if you are applying for a job by letter.

Analyze Your Prospect's Needs,
Show How You Fit In

Before you write one word, plan your whole campaign. Find out something about the company, if you are not familiar with it, then analyze the prospect's needs. Everything you say and do should point toward supplying his needs, doing him good — at the same time that it flatters his judgment. It helps if you have an angle or a dramatic approach that sets your letter apart, but you must put in some meat in addition.

The following is similar to a letter I once wrote which got me an immediate telephone call with a request for an interview.

Dear Mr. Owner:

Yours is a big store and a beautiful store. Don't you think it is time you started doing big store advertising?

With my experience and skills I believe that I can help you to get a great deal more out of your advertising dollar — a better image for your fine store, and bigger sales of the items advertised. One secret is pro-rating advertising costs; another is better presentation.

I have made up a few layouts, using some of the merchandise featured in your recent ads, and I should like very much to show them to you. They illustrate the principles I am talking about. I can arrange to see you at any time that is convenient to you. My telephone number is 000-0000.

Respectfully,

(Signature)

I was taking a calculated risk in my opening line. The man might have loved the advertising he was doing, or he might even have been doing it himself. (I found out that he was not, before I wrote my letter.) I hoped to overcome any possibility of arousing antagonism by using the powerful appeals of more-for-your-money and bigger sales. It worked like a charm. The man had no sooner read the letter than he telephoned me, and I eventually got the job.

The letter is brief, and yet there is a great deal in it. I not only tell Mr. Owner that I will get him more for his money, but I give some brief, professionally phrased examples of how I will do it. I tell him I have experience and skills, and then I offer to prove it, with actual layouts using his own merchandise. By this device I also show him that I have studied his store individually. The fact that I have already done the layouts shows him that I am not afraid of work, not afraid to put my knowledge on the line. I also appeal to his vanity. Nearly every business owner wants to believe that his is an impressive outfit. My opening line tells him that I appreciate his store and I want to help others to appreciate it.

This is the way good letters are constructed. They put the message across, but they convey much of it indirectly.

Of course, there are other good approaches. Sometimes the mere listing of your experience, if it is outstanding, is enough to get you an interview. In using this method, the listing should be tabulated. Once again, your approach should be directed toward what you can do to benefit the prospective employer.

Avoid Sending a Resume

Especially if you are approaching a prospective employer cold turkey, I believe you should avoid presenting a standard resume until after the first interview. This is not always possible, with business practices becoming more and more standardized, but often it is. In these instances I believe you can achieve a better effect by using some of the resume material in a letter. You can use the material as selling ammunition. Here is an example:

Dear Mr. Prospect:

As sales manager for a leading manufacturing firm, I put in a system that increased sales by 15 percent the first year, with consistent gains thereafter. Through cutting of costs, average profit on all sales was increased by 3 percent.

You may be interested in a man with my sales management experience and organizing ability. It is possible that some slight changes might increase profits for your corporation. Here are some other things I have accomplished:

— Opened up new markets by uncovering new uses for products, resulting in additional sales of $3 million.

— Hired and trained new salesmen in methods that helped them become the top producers of the company sales staff.

— Campaigned for trademark identity among consumers for an oldline product, increasing demand by 30 percent. Volume grew from $16 million to $37 million in four years.

I should like very much to meet you and discuss further details of my experience.

Very truly yours,

Remember, every business has problems of one sort or another all the time. A letter that seems to promise answers to some problems — and especially the problem of making or saving money — is likely to receive attention. This is a much better approach than writing a noncommittal letter and enclosing a buckshot resume.

Avoid submitting a resume unless you are absolutely compelled to. Never mail one. You should write the resume, fully and completely — but for your own use only. Excerpt it for the purpose of writing letters that cover only the sort of experience that is applicable. Later, if a resume must be furnished, use your basic resume to make up a revised one that is tailor-made for the particular situation.

Follow-Up Can Make the Difference in Selling Yourself

Whether you are applying for a job by letter or in person, follow-up is important. If the follow-up is a letter, make it a revised version of your first letter, possibly introducing a new slant or new material. If you were interviewed in person, try to leave the way open to come back when you cannot clinch the matter on the first visit. Use similar phrases and methods to those recommended for salesmen earlier in this chapter.

If, by chance, you are actually in the market for a job at this time, run, do not walk, to the nearest library or book store and get yourself a copy of Carl Boll's book, *"Executive Jobs Unlimited."* It is the finest book I have ever read on the subject of getting a job. Boll is a proven expert, and goes into the process in great detail.

CHAPTER 16

Keeping Your Eye on The Ball—For Constant Advancement

Think, think, think — be prepared ahead of time for any tricky situation that may arise. This, perhaps, is the major message of this book, and you are given the keys to guide your thinking and behavior.

As you studied the book and committed the important phrases to memory, you may have noticed that the use of these tools for putting yourself across requires self-discipline. If you have always been an impulsive person, you may feel that in following these principles you will be forced to play a part. True enough. However, as you discover the magic of the key words and phrases, their use and the attitudes behind them will become second nature. You will have grown. You will be on your way, girded and armed for the upward climb, at ease in any company.

Prepare in Order to Take Command

Remember always that impulsiveness and the privilege of reacting thoughtlessly to another's acts or words are not true freedom. Actually these are signs that you are not in command of yourself or the situation. You are not making the positive choice of the path you will take, but are simply reacting to another person's words or behavior — perhaps allowing him by indirection to send you down the rocky chute to oblivion.

If there is one motto the ambitious man should engrave on his mind, it is "Keep your eye on the ball." This is the keystone of success. In every business situation, keep in mind what it is that you want to accomplish — the goal of the moment, and the long-term goal. Have your arsenal of key words and phrases ready to save you when impatience or a flare of temper might enter in and shove you off the path. You must abstain from a few primitive pleasures in favor of the private joy of knowing you are managing things, putting yourself on the road to success.

When anger flares and discussions become dangerously heated, certain phrases we have already discussed are particularly helpful. The "stalling for time" phrases give pause and steer minds back into reasonable channels. Try any of these:

- In a situation like this, there are several points of view to be considered.
- Well, certainly there is much truth in what each of us has said. Let's write down the various points and discuss them one by one.
- In studying all sides of the question, I believe we will find there is much to be said on both sides. For my part, I rather lean toward . . ..
- It's true that such and such is the case . . . (repeating others' points, and then leading into yours).

By stalling, by speaking calmly, you can tame any impulse you might have had toward exasperation, or you can lead yourself into re-phrasing a comment into a constructive form.

If you find you need even more time to subdue a fit of temper, try the long-deferment approach. You might say:

- I would like to give this matter some study and give you a full report.
- I don't believe we should make a snap judgment on this. I would be interested to hear Blank Department's views on the matter.
- I think we should have Bill White's opinion on this before making any decision.

The momentary distraction of the discussions engendered should give you time to overcome any impulsive, destructive urge you might have had. If the chairman decides not to defer decision, you will have gotten command of yourself and will be ready with an acceptable approach.

A Seeming Exception

Occasionally, people who inherit money or who accidentally fall into a winning situation appear to ignore the prerequisite that you must control yourself in order to control your future. Actually they do not. Inept, undisciplined characters fumble onward for a time, protected by their money or connections, but they limit themselves all along the way, and often end up in utter defeat.

A man I know is an example of this. He was a tall, very handsome young man, one of those with innate charm — charisma, if you will. He also was fairly intelligent and an ambitious, hard worker. We'll call him Jim Peterson, which is not his name.

Jim graduated from college as an engineer during the Great Depression. He found that engineers were a dime a dozen at that time and opportunities nil, so he took the first job that luck and charm presented him. He became a salesman in a giant department store, and he worked hard at the job. His record and outstanding appearance soon attracted the attention of the general manager.

Wutherington, the manager (not his real name), had always wanted a son, and he made Peterson his protege. Within a year or two Peterson became a divisional manager. This was no small job but he did quite well, due in large degree to the checks and balances in a giant store's pattern of organization, and due not a little to the protection of the general manager.

All well and good. Jim Peterson might have gone on forever in this special setup, but the general manager was also ambitious, and he set about buying a store of his own. He took Peterson with him to the new department store, giving him a fat salary and a good share of the corporate stock. Peterson was in clover, riding around in a chauffeured Cadillac, brandishing fifty cent cigars, traveling to Europe and the Orient regularly with his patron on buying trips.

Peterson thought he had it made, and so did everyone else; then his patron died, taken with a massive heart attack. Suddenly Peterson was on his own, deprived of his protected environment. He was thrown into the position of having to get along with someone who did not love him, and he did not know how. In fact, he did not even realize the necessity of making the effort.

It turned out that old man Wutherington had left 60 percent of the store's voting stock to a nephew, and enough to Peterson to give his protege a generous 40 percent. The 60 percent put the nephew in charge, and this man was determined to exercise his rights. From the start he infuriated Peterson by going over all the books and buying methods, asking questions as he went. Then, unimpressed by grand gestures and aging charisma, he sheared away a great deal of Jim's authority.

Lack of Control Destroys A Career

One day Peterson could stand no more. He flared up and shouted at his tormenter, "I don't have to take orders from you!"

"You'll either take orders from me or get out of the business," the younger Wutherington announced. Peterson had created a senseless impasse that patience and skilled use of the key words and phrases would almost surely have avoided. He ended up selling out to Wutherington for a relative pittance, because he could not wait to be out of the embarrassing situation.

The case of Peterson is extreme, but many a lesser such personal tragedy is acted out every day. Sometimes it involves the fate of others as well.

Train Your Help in the Key Words and Phrases

A friend of mine was telling me of a disastrous experience he just went through with a new secretary. Bob Jones, we'll call him, was recently promoted from school principal to a much larger managerial post. His job now is to organize a new department in the educational system of a great eastern city. Such an undertaking is always a ticklish business, because it changes old ways, realigns some authority, creates new guidelines. Zealous defenders of their time-honored grooves are always ready to do battle in such a situation, and to throw in a timely monkey wrench. Yet their cooperation is necessary to the formation of the new department, and to the success of it.

Treading softly, yet skillfully, Bob had been receiving excellent cooperation from officials and other department managers. Then he was forced to hire a new secretary! (His old one had left the city.)

Technical Skills Alone Won't Do

The new woman, selected by the Personnel Department, was superb in her typing and shorthand skills, but after a week on the job she had wreaked such havoc in personal relations that Bob is beginning to wonder if he can ever repair the damage. The woman was fired, of course, but the ill-will she has created in her short stay lives on.

How different these two situations could have been if the

two people involved in the wrecking jobs had just kept their eyes on the ball.

If Peterson had kept his eyes glued to his objective, if he had learned self-discipline and even a few of the key words and phrases, he might have gone on to new glory instead of defeat. When his patron died and the collapse of his dreams faced him, Peterson should have sat down and said to himself, "Let me consider all possibilities of what may occur, and let me plan to cope with them. *First of all, what do I want to achieve?*"

Bob Jones' secretary should have known that any secretary's main objective is to promote her superior's objectives. She must:

- Keep the peace.
- Make friends.
- Oil the wheels of the business machinery.

If this young woman had done this, kept her eye on the ball, she might still have been on her way to the top with an executive headed for the top.

Your Aides Are You

For his part, Bob Jones may have learned a valuable lesson. That is, so far as your contacts are concerned, your aides are YOU. They, as well as you, must say and do the right thing at the right time to protect your image and theirs. A new secretary or any assistant must have your aims explained and must be carefully supervised. He or she should be introduced to the major key words and phrases, not neglecting "Please," "Thank you," "I'll be glad to," or "I would be glad to, but . . . ," and "It's a pleasure." A new employee's reactions during a few indoctrination sessions may clue one in on weaknesses and forestall much damage. Never take it for granted that all secretaries come ready-equipped with tact.

"What do I want to achieve?" This is the question that anyone who works with others should ask himself constantly, and all his words, all his actions, should be directed toward this prime objective. To quote the famous words of Ty Cobb, "If you can't see it, you can't hit it." Make yourself see it, and keep your eye on the ball.

Trading New Habits for Old

Again, if you have never tried this approach to living, it may seem difficult, and yet it can become second nature. It is simply a matter of substituting good habits for bad ones. Once you have committed to memory the key words and phrases, more than half the battle is won.

In the beginning you may have to paste a disciplinary phrase in your hat, write it on your cuff, or place it in the lid of your cigarette case. Either one of the two disciplinary phrases will do: "Keep your eye on the ball," or "Remember what I want to achieve."

Read the admonition over five, ten, or fifty times a day if necessary. When a situation begins to get tense or you feel your temper rising, read your motto. It will work wonders.

Take Time Out to Plan
for Advancement

For your day to day happiness and peace of mind, next in importance to keeping your job is the feeling that you are going some place — that you are getting ahead. It is a feeling you can always have, *if you know where you are going.* Few people in this world have the good fortune to be wafted upward willy-nilly as Peterson was, and perhaps he was not lucky that success came early without planning. How much more fortunate is the man or woman who can say, "I carved my own way to success, and if I should have reversals here and there, I know how to get out of them."

Such a person has a valid image of himself as a success — not some hazy dream of wealth and indolence — but a true, well-etched image. He got where he was by holding to this image and proceeding according to plan. The key words and phrases will help you on your way, but it is vital to decide early just where it is that you want to go. You must decide what your long-term objective will be, and then you must plan how to get there. As a start, ask yourself, "What will be the first step upward?"

Suppose you are a salesman. Your long-term objective may be to become sales-manager, or it may be even more distant. You may decide that you want to be general manager of the company.

Just stating the objective is more planning than most people do, but if you really want to get ahead you should plan the steps upward one by one, and analyze what knowledge and abilities will be required. Face the facts squarely. Before going further, give yourself this quiz:

1. Do you want to acquire the knowledge necessary?
2. What schooling will be required?
3. Will you go through with this necessary schooling?
4. Have you the brains?
5. Have you the ambition and stamina required for the background work and the climb?
6. Will family obligations permit time for the schooling and training?
7. Will your mate agree willingly to the sacrifices necessary?

If the answer to any of these questions is no, then you had better change your goal to something realistic, something you can achieve with the amount of effort you can expend. (You can always revise your goal upward, if it later seems practicable.)

Having decided definitely on your ultimate goal, then you must decide what step number 1 is on the climb — your immediate aim. Steps number 2 and 3 should also be thought of. It may help in your planning to make a chart for yourself, showing the possible routes to the top. (This chart is not something you will paste on your wall, or discuss with anyone. Writing it down is recommended only as a means to help you clarify your thoughts.)

Further Test Yourself

Day to day you will chiefly be concerned only with the next step on the way. Of prime importance in your plan is to be topnotch in your present job. If you are a salesman, for instance, then plan to be the best salesman in the group. Analyze what it is that makes a great salesman.

After you have written down the attributes that make up the picture, test your own behavior and accomplishments against the list. Be objective. You will doubtless see one or more areas where you can improve.

Here is one list, but it is only a suggestion. See if you can add to it, or better yet, make up your own.

**Example: Necessary Qualifications
of a Great Salesman**

1. Likes people, is friendly.
2. People are friendly to him.
3. Is not shy.
4. Inspires confidence.
5. Is aggressive without being annoying.
6. Knows how to joke and remembers jokes.
7. Is a good judge of people.
8. Is generous without being extravagant.
9. Knows his product or products thoroughly.
   a. Knows all selling points and advantages.
   b. Knows the answers to all objections.
10. Is good at record-keeping.
11. Is punctual.
12. Is patient when necessary.
13. Is not a clock-watcher.
14. Is a self-starter.
15. Knows how to close a sale.
16. Knows how to create another chance when a brush-off threatens.

Merely working on such a list is bound to be helpful, because it sets you to analyzing your job, to approaching it scientifically, rather than just blundering through it. Your job and all phases of it will become more interesting.

In addition to thinking and analyzing on your own, start reading. There is much literature, for instance, devoted to the selling field. One book a month should be immensely helpful, simply because it keeps you thinking, keeps you examining your approach. Remember, any job you have, no matter what it is, is an opportunity. It may be only the preliminary step on the upward climb, but it is a step. Once you realize this, you are on your way.

"But," you may protest, "I don't like the job I am in!"

All the more reason to do that job well — if only to be promoted out of it. I was once promoted out of a hated job in two days, simply by breaking all records in accomplishing it!

Go Beyond the Call of Duty

Once you have made your initial plan of procedure for getting ahead, do not discard it. Keep it and review it periodically — as often as every week. This will help you to keep your goal in mind, and will re-impress on you the importance of the key words and phrases for putting yourself across.

As you work from day to day, doing the best job of which you are capable, look for opportunities to subtly show that you can look beyond your job, and that you have management's good at heart. In this latter connection, everyone knows the importance of saying "we" in discussing the company's problems and objectives. It still holds true. The mere fact of saying "We could do this," or "We could do that," indicates that you consider yourself part of the company, and that you intend to stay with it.

As for demonstrating what you can do above and beyond your job, there are many avenues. One way is to jot down a memorandum to yourself every time you are irritated by something that is inefficient, or every time you think of a better way to do things. Give these matters lots of thought, then try to think of solutions. Check your ideas for feasibility and possible objectionable features. When you are sure you have a reasonably good suggestion to make, carefully present it.

Method and Timing Important —
Suggested Approaches

A word of caution may be needed here, and that is: Do not go over your immediate boss' head with these suggestions, or he may think you are trying for HIS job. Either present your ideas to him, or, if it can be gracefully and logically done, present them in a general meeting.

Proceed with caution, also, in choosing the proper time to put forth your suggestions. Wait for the auspicious opportunity.

If you are a salesman, you might say to your sales-manager over a cup of coffee, "Clyde, you know the problem we've been having with deliveries from Chicago? Well, I've been thinking about it, and I believe it might be because we send the orders all in for delivery on the first of the month. I wonder if it wouldn't be a good idea to have two delivery dates — say, the first and the fifteenth. I know the shipping cost would be greater, but the way I figure it, we might actually save money. You have to count all the time that is lost in follow-ups and the foul-ups with duplicate orders — not to mention the infuriated customers. Why don't we try the two dates? Is there any real reason against it? It would smooth out the rush period in Chicago."

Even better timing would be to wait until Clyde mentions the problem, if he is likely to, and then present your idea.

Clyde may tell you there is a good reason why your plan is not workable. Still, he will appreciate your interest in the problem, and you will have raised your head above the crowd. On the other hand, Clyde may use the suggestion and benefit you, himself, and the company. This particular suggestion, incidentally, was proved out by one of the world's largest cosmetic companies. For years they scheduled deliveries for once a month. When they switched to twice a month, sales almost doubled and operations were smoother.

One art director I knew in a large advertising agency used a unique way to show that he could go beyond the good job he already had. Instead of just roughing in nonsense or black lines in preliminary layouts, he usually thought of a clever copy idea and used that instead. He took a bit of ribbing for it, but the headlines did not pass unnoticed. The payoff came several years later, when he was made director of the entire agency operation.

Enlarging your horizons, learning to think big, is an important part of the art of keeping your eye on the ball.

Presenting an Idea — Useful Phrases to Practice

Phrases for presenting ideas can only be guidelines. Occasionally you may use one as is, but more often you will have to adapt and vary slightly to suit the situation. Nevertheless, you will find it useful to have these phrases in the back of your mind. Remember, too, that the manner of presentation is important as well as the words. Make sure there is no touch of arrogance or superiority, or you are likely to arouse opposition rather than appreciation. Be a little hesitant, a little modest. Above all, do not project the idea that you are discontented with your present post.

Here are a few suggested openings. Note how casual and easily phrased they are. Some have an air of spontaneity. Read the phrases aloud and practice them a few times.

- There must be a solution to our problem . . . What do you think of this idea?
- Why don't we do a little brainstorming on this problem? I have a couple of thoughts, and maybe some other people do, too. (In this case you are prepared, while others are probably not. It embodies a bit of one-upmanship.)
- You know what I think, J. G.? I think there might be some shortcuts we could take in this process (or

a better way we could do this). Why don't we think this through — discuss it a bit?

- I had a brainstorm last night on this situation. I don't know whether my idea is any good or not, but I'd like to tell you about it. If it is workable, it might save us quite a bit of money. Here — I've made a few notes (or drawn up a couple of charts).

Don't Go Off Half-Cocked

Taking the casual approach in presenting your ideas or suggestions does not mean that you should treat the ideas lightly or be sloppy in the presentation. It is important to develop ideas fully and think them through. If charts are needed for a convincing presentation, make the charts, and have them as neat and professional-looking as you can. If figures and statistics are necessary, research them carefully and have them accurate. Such things as floor plans or maps should be done to accurate scale. (See Chapter Thirteen.)

These physical adjuncts to idea-presentation have many virtues. They help to clarify your own thinking, and they are something tangible for another to fix his mind upon. Beyond this, they are impressive physical evidence of the work and thought you have contributed. It goes without saying, of course, that you should never present a continuing flood of these things. Use judgment. Watch reactions.

Note also that the foregoing stress on care and thoroughness applies to your planned presentations. Do not let this deter you from participating freely in brainstorming sessions, where off-the-cuff ideas are wanted.

Let This Book Keep
You on the Track

Now that we come to the close of this book, let us consider how best it can serve you.

Like the auto mechanic's manual, "How to Put Yourself Across With Key Words and Phrases" is not a one-time thing. It is a handbook to guide you from day to day in the complex processes of engineering your success. Do not put this book in the bookcase. Keep it on the table beside your favorite chair, or keep it on your night stand, if you read in bed.

Whenever you are up against a problem at work or are considering an important maneuver, look over the table of contents and re-read the chapter that applies.

In forming new, constructive habits, especially when they are habits of thinking and reaction, it is important to impress upon the mind, over and over again, the lessons that are needed. Do not wait until you have made a mistake and then try frantically to repair the damage. Keep yourself primed and ready to head off old bad habits.

In addition to using your handbook as a ready-reference guide, make it a point to re-read the entire book every two or three months as a refresher course. Mark on your desk calendar special dates for this re-reading. Each time you go through the book, new points will be emphasized in your mind and you will come away more confident, better prepared for the executive climb. Putting yourself across will become a constant subtle facet of your behavior at all times.

INDEX

Index